Unlawful Flight:
A Parental Kidnapping

A Memoir

Unlawful Flight:
A Parental Kidnapping

A Memoir

By Glen C. Schulz

WindBlown Books

www.unlawfulflight.com

For further information, please contact:
glen@unlawfulflight.com

WindBlown Books
P.O.Box 721683
Houston, TX 77272-1683

Book design by:

Arbor Books Inc.
www.arborbooks.com

Printed in the United States

Unlawful Flight: A Parental Kidnapping
Glen C. Schulz

Library of Congress Control Number: 2006934820

ISBN 10: 0-9789923-0-X
ISBN 13: 978-0-9789923-0-9

DEDICATION

I did not write this book to get your sympathy, nor beg your forgiveness. I wrote it because this story needed to be told. I wrote it for all of the people out there who think that the world is full of heartless, uncaring, ruthless people. It is also for those who choose to believe that there is no God. This book was written to show all of those people that they are mistaken. My story is proof that good people are out there everywhere and that without question, there is a God and all you have to do is believe and ask for help. I did.

This book is also a tribute to all of the schoolteachers in our world. They can only do so much with their hands tied by laws and the fear of lawsuits and yet they instinctively lead our young towards all that is right, one way or another.

Lastly, this book is dedicated to the memory of my parents, Daphne and Marvin Schulz. Without their love and support I would have no story to write. I will see them again one day, I'm absolutely sure of it.

TABLE OF CONTENTS

INTRODUCTION

On the evening of Friday, August 7th, 1981, for the first time in two months, I could legally go to my home and pick up my two children for the weekend. Finally the law was on my side and my wife had no choice but to let me see them. The joy on our faces was blatantly obvious and very upsetting to her.

She pushed a finger into my chest in a last act of spitefulness and said, "You have them back here Sunday by 6 P.M. you bastard, or I'll never let you see them again." I quickly smiled and said "Yes, ma'am," knowing deep down inside that if all went well she would be the one that would never see us again. It was a broad smile that came easily that evening. Not only was I getting to see my children for the first time in a very long time, I was about to change all of our lives in one short weekend. And it was the first time in what seemed like an eternity that I had reason to smile.

At one o'clock in the morning on Sunday, August 9th, I carried my two sleeping children from my parents' house to the van waiting out in the driveway, laid them on sleeping bags and we were gone. I told no one where we were going. I couldn't risk it. We headed to the last place that I expected anyone would ever think to look for us. That was my first mistake. About six weeks later I was climbing over a fence at the back of a Phoenix car dealership while the police were in the office at the front.

And about 10 days after that, in a motel room in Van Horn, Texas, I flipped a nickel to decide whether we were going to go to Dallas or Houston. It made no difference to me whatsoever; I didn't know one soul in the entire state. It landed tails. Decided by the flip of a nickel in a little town that we had never heard of, we were going to start new lives once again, this time in Houston and I was the only person on planet earth that knew it! I quickly learned from my prior mistake and used an assumed name until I could no longer pull it off and I saved as much money as I could, knowing full well that the shit would hit the fan one day and I had better be prepared. But until then we would have the time of our lives and we would enjoy every minute of every day, the three of us always aware that it could be our last day together. The future would hold many surprises for us, from fear to love, from handcuffs to happiness, help from the most unlikely sources and unques-tioned support from everyone we met.

DISCLAIMER

What I did so many years ago was wrong and I do *not* in any way condone or encourage anyone to ever do it. I did it because I wanted my children to be happy and I believed it to be the only way that I could make that happen. I knew that it was wrong and that I could spend years in prison if things didn't go our way. And yet with the odds stacked heavily against us we were so lucky, so fortunate and we will be forever grateful to everyone involved that helped us, whether they did it knowingly or not. This story is written the way that I remember it and with using all of the pieces of our past that I still have and hold near and dear to me. It happened a long time ago. Most of the names have been changed to protect their privacy and for legal reasons.

CHAPTER ONE:
A LITTLE BACKGROUND

Sandy and I met when we both worked at a truck stop in Kingsville, Ohio, back in the spring of 1970. I had just turned 17 and she was 20. We dated a few times while we continued to date others as well. One of the others that she dated was Steve Hill, my best friend and longtime school buddy who also worked at the truck stop. Steve and I were both still in school and both seniors at Northwestern High School in Albion, Pennsylvania. Sandy had already graduated. She dated both of us on and off for a while at first and I quickly began to fall in love with her. She was the kind of person that lived for the moment, each moment a separate time in her life and I liked that most of all about her. But her way to live life was what I would now call a rollercoaster effect, excited and happy at times and then down and depressed at other times. She came from a poor family and she worked a teletype machine at the truck stop, relaying messages between trucking companies and their drivers. Steve and I worked the diesel pumps. As time went on Sandy told Steve she was falling in love with me and that she would not be seeing him anymore. He was pretty upset about it and became jealous as hell. That created some serious animosity between Steve and me, even though we had been best friends for many years.

That August I was going to England for the whole month with my family. We weren't wealthy people; my mother was born in Jersey, one of the Channel Islands off the southern coast of England. When the Germans occupied the Islands during World War II, mother and her family immigrated to England along with almost everyone else, leaving behind everything they owned and traveling by way of anything that could float. The family settled in Weymouth, Dorset, on the southern coast and mother eventually became a nurse's aide during the war. My father met her at a Dance in Weymouth, England, in 1946 while he was serving in the Marine Corps. Dad came home after his military service and saved all of his money so that he could bring mom over as soon as possible. In 1948, mother said goodbye to her family and her way of life and sailed alone to Baltimore, Maryland, and the great United States. They married and settled in Waterford, Pennsylvania, where my father was born. That was all in 1948. My mother was going home for the very first time since she had left and except for the oldest two children, the rest of our family was going with her.

We were gone the entire month and the very night we came back, Steve showed up at the house and began to tell me just what a slut Sandy had been while I was gone. He said that he had seen her around town with several different guys and that because we were friends he wanted me to know about it. I did what anyone would have done, I got pissed off and punched him and told him to get the hell out of my sight. Steve and I have never once spoken since that night. At the time I thought that he was just trying to bust us up out of pure jealousy, but later on I would learn that most of what he was telling me had been the truth.

Sandy and I continued our relationship after the trip; in fact, she came to the house soon after Steve left that first night I was back. I asked her about what she did while I was gone and she said she did nothing but wait for me and I chose to believe her.

We began to date constantly and we were always together when we were not at work. And every time that I wound up alone with her father he would ask me when I was going to marry her and get her the hell out of his life. He was a (I'm not going to go there), and he had not held a real job for many years. The only income in their family was from Sandy and her mother, Norma, an amazing woman born with one good arm and a stub for the other. Because John drank excessively and could not keep a job, Norma, out of necessity, became the breadwinner and John opted to do nothing to help anyone. It was a screwed up family and I should have known that there were going to be big problems later.

So I believe now that we were pushed into an early marriage, mostly by her parents; they wanted her to grab onto me and never let go because they thought that my father was wealthy and therefore, I was. They were of course wrong, but they were going on the assumption that if we could afford to go to England for a month, heck, we must be rich. Anyway, in 1971, I had to ask my father if I could marry Sandy because in Pennsylvania you had to be 21 years old to marry unless you had permission from your parents. Dads' response was not only no, it was hell no.

In September of 1971, my sister Linda was marrying Mike Michelini, her longtime boyfriend and Sandy's family was now pushing us hard to have a double wedding with them; but never wavering, my father said he wouldn't allow it. I asked my sister if she would try to talk Dad into allowing it, but she showed little or no interest at all in helping me. I found out later that she didn't approve of Sandy, although she had never said anything to me about it. I also found out later that Linda had seen Sandy with other guys while I was gone. Sandy and I looked at our options and the only one we had was to elope. Our mindset was that we'd show them that they couldn't stop

us, hell, you can't stop true love. And so with a little homework, we found that North Carolina had no waiting period; if
you could prove you were old enough, they would marry you.
In late October, we drove to Sparta, North Carolina, and just
before we were married, I called my father to tell him where we
were and what we were going to do. Dad asked me not to do
it; he said that if we came back he would allow a wedding and
we could marry at a local church. I thanked him but said after
driving this far, we were going to go through with it. And we
did. After picking up the marriage license in a clerk's office, I
grabbed Sandy and kissed her, thinking the license made us
legally married and I wasn't waiting another minute to kiss my
wife. Several of the clerks laughed and advised me that we were
not yet man and wife, that we had to go see the preacher next
door and make it official. So, we went next door and got in
line. Minutes later we were wed with the preachers' family as
witnesses. It was October 23rd, 1971. Just after the ceremony,
I asked the preacher how much I owed him and he responded
by asking me how much she was worth. I gave him 40 bucks.

There was a small reception for us after our return to
Conneaut following a brief honeymoon at her sister's home in
Saint Charles, Missouri. The reception was held at a bar down
in the harbor area of Conneaut; you guessed it, her father
picked the place. And when we opened our wedding gifts we
came across a card that had my father's handwriting on it. I
opened the card and inside it was a note with a check. The note
read, "Here is a check for every dollar we ever took from you
and all the interest it has earned over the years. You will need it
much more now than you thought you needed it when we took
it from you. We are sorry that you were so mad at us for all
these years because of it." But I'm getting ahead of myself.

I will never forget our first Christmas. We were living in a
duplex on Buffalo Street in Conneaut, Ohio. We had pur-

chased a color television months earlier on layaway at a Kmart in Erie, Pennsylvania: a Panasonic 19-inch, state-of-the-art beauty. We did without a lot of fun things so that we could pay it off and have the television by the time we married. It was one of the few things that we had in our barren apartment that was ours alone, no hand-me-down from someone else. We were proud of it, a color television, and it was paid for! We set up our hand-me-down aluminum Christmas tree with the multicolored rotating wheel that turns completely around, making the tree different colors. We had nothing but each other and our new television, and yet it was enough. It was going to be a great first Christmas together.

And then the call came, Sandy and a girlfriend had been arrested in Ashtabula for theft at a department store. The husband of the other girl was in a panic when he called because they had four children and he needed her out of jail right away but he had no money to bond her out with. I didn't either, nor did I even know what a bond was. But within 12 hours Sandy and her friend were out of jail and we were minus our new television set. We never saw it again.

Sandy and I lived in Ohio at first; later moving to Massachusetts in 1972 so that I could work at a General Motors assembly plant in Framingham. Her brother Bob was working there and he said that he thought he could get me in. So we moved out of Ohio and in with Bob and his wife, Anna, and their two children, sharing their apartment in Holliston. It took a while to get in at the assembly plant and so I worked at a glove manufacturing company at first. Bob and Anna were great people and I know how many times they fought because we were in that apartment with them, cramping them to where they had to keep their kids in their own bedroom so we could have a bedroom of our own. It was awful tight and I know how hard it was for all of us. We were there for a little over half a year when Bob and Anna had their third child, a son. They bought a home and moved out after that and we took over the lease of the apartment. It was at 35 Katherine Lane, Apartment 3B, in Holliston, Massachusetts. I had a good job, making good money and Sandy took a job as a waitress at a bar in Hopkinton to help us get ahead. I worked the second shift at General Motors, the 5:30pm to 2:30am shift. Sandy worked until the bar closed and we usually got home about the same time. We had the good life and in the early part of 1973, Sandy became pregnant. We were thrilled. Life was just great. I can still remember the time that Sandy and I got to see Roberta Flack sing her "Killing Me Softly" song in Boston. Even now I can remember how wonderful she sang and how much the words meant to me. I felt that way about Sandy.

We had everything we wanted and to top it off, our first child, a boy, was born in Natick, Massachusetts in October of 1973. With Brian healthy, we were on top of the world; that is until the Arab oil embargo happened and we were all waiting in lines for hours to buy gasoline. Soon after, the gas-guzzler cars stopped selling and General Motors began to lay off thousands. I was one of them. Our world crumbled a bit. Life wasn't so easy all of a sudden. It was an awakening to the real world.

We moved back to Ohio in the spring of 1974 and found an apartment above a doctor's office. I collected sub benefits for a while from General Motors and thanks to an old friend of Sandy's; I got a part-time job driving a semi truck, delivering tin cans for a local company. I would be gone two days at a time and would get about $90 for each trip, but it was only once a week and hardly worth it. And I found out driving a semi truck in the snow sucks. I hated it. Try driving a big rig up a snow-covered hill only to start sliding backward before you make it to the top. All you professional drivers know what I'm talking about and you're right, you don't get paid enough! But there was not a lot of opportunity back then. The steel industry, the biggest employer in the area, was going down and more and more people were being laid off and looking for work.

Luckily I found another job, at Olin Matheson, a chemical company in Ashtabula, Ohio. I worked as a painter, hanging off of large towers sandblasting and spray painting whatever they wanted painted. It was while I was working there that my daughter Melissa was born, in July 1975. I got the phone call while at work; "Sandy's about to have the baby," they said. I flew out of there and headed the 10 miles to the hospital in Conneaut. It was quite a trip. I was quickly pulled over for speeding in Kingsville, Ohio. By the time the police officer got out of his car, I was already out and running towards him. He pulled out his gun, pointed it at me and ordered me back to my car, scaring the hell out of me. I told him that my wife was having a baby at Brown Memorial Hospital in Conneaut and that was why I was in such a hurry.

He made a call on his radio and came back to me and said, "Ever had a police escort before?" I remember smiling as I said "hell no." The cop smiled back and said, "Just follow me." It was awesome! He hauled ass to the hospital with lights and siren on and I was speeding along right behind him. We were both grinning from ear to ear when we pulled into the hospital parking lot. I shook his hand while saying thank you and ran into the building as he yelled good luck. I waited in the waiting room alone because it was a small hospital and it was late, and after the phone rang for about the one hundredth time, I answered it by saying that there was no one manning the desk. "Mr. Schulz would you like to come up and see your daughter?" the doctor asked. I raced upstairs to see her. She was wonderful, a healthy, beautiful baby girl, my baby girl. My Melissa.

By the following year I was working in the parts department at Harris and Sergeant Ford, a dealership in Albion,
Pennsylvania. I took this job after the painter position fizzled
at the plant in Ashtabula; once you paint everything you're not
needed anymore and we were laid off. I was working the parts
counter there when a man came in to order parts for the cars
he was repairing. His name was Bob Leehan, owner of Leehan
Auto Body, in Cranesville, Pennsylvania. He and I became
friends and one day he asked if I knew of anyone that would
be interested in learning his trade because he needed a helper.
I raised my hand and said, "Me."

To make a long story short, I wound up working in his little body shop as a helper, learning whatever I could so that I
would wind up with a trade. Talk about having it all, I was the
father of two healthy children and I was doing well learning a
trade that paid well if you were good at it. My father had
always said; "a real trade will last you a lifetime." Looking back
now that it is 2004 and I am the manager of a very large Lexus
body shop, I know just how right he was.

We lived above the doctors' office, so each fall or cut or ill-
ness was just a run down the stairs to get treated. One day,
Brian hit the gate at the top of the stairs in his roll-around
walker, knocking the gate down, and tumbling down about 16
steps. He literally landed in the doctor's office. Doctor Doran
was holding him by the time we reached the bottom stairs. It
doesn't get any better than that! Brian took a few stitches to his
upper lip and he was as good as new.

Sandy came from a poor family and did not need a lot to
keep her happy and I was easy to please, a family to come
home to and some coffee pretty much did it for me. The few
times that we needed something and had no means to get it, I
would borrow from my father. You know the plan, where you
borrow from dad when you have to and then plan on paying

it back, but never do. I didn't do this often, in fact, I was too proud to ask for help. I had been raised that way. Years later I would have to learn to swallow that pride over and over again just to keep my children with me.

After working for Bob for a year I had learned enough to ask for a raise and Bob looked me right in the eye and said, "I wish I could give you one, you've earned it, but I can't afford to." He was telling me the truth, he couldn't afford to, not with the 10 kids that he had. He said that he wanted me to stay, but he would understand if I had to go. With two kids of my own and just barely making ends meet, we both knew I would have to go.

It was somewhere about then that Sandy began to say little things to me about how life was in some way disappointing her; we were not achieving the things that she had hoped for. We didn't have the money to buy the things and do the things and go to the places that she was beginning to want. At first it was subtle hints and I took them directly to heart. I was letting her down, but we were gaining ground just like every other young couple out there. She was belittling me because I wasn't what her family had thought I was, wealthy. And she was realizing that if she wanted to distance herself from her poor past, I wasn't going to be her ticket to wealth and material things. Over time Sandy got much better at belittling me and cared less and less about who was around when she did.

I stopped one morning at one of the largest independent body shops in Conneaut, Ohio. I walked in, asked for the owner and a tall, thin man named George Laituri introduced himself to me and said that he was the owner. I told him who I was, what I thought I could do for him, and whom I was currently working for. His eyes lit up when I told him Bob Leehan had taught me the trade. He asked me if I could do framework and weld. "Yes," I told him and he hired me on the spot. I gave

Bob two weeks notice and then started with George, it was much closer to home and more money too.

Our lives were good. I was making better money and things were good with Sandy and the kids. We had a lot of fun together. We would go to the lake and swim, have picnics with family and friends, even go to Sea World and / or Geauga Lake in Aurora, Ohio, every year; sometimes even Cedar Point, in Sandusky. Sandy was a good mother and a good wife and I had no complaints. My parents loved her a great deal. Everyone in my family liked her, that is, except my sister. Linda always had a way of seeing through people and she could tell right from the first time she had met Sandy that something wasn't right, she could smell it. My sister has always been there for me through every twist in my entire life. She is my only sister; I have five brothers and her. I always tell her that she is my favorite sister. Anyway, she was my protector and friend and I, hers. In earlier years, we had double-dated and tried to watch out for each other and we had a kind of special bond that sometimes forms. As sweet as all that sounds, it was not without motive, if she wanted to do something or go somewhere, Dad would normally say no unless I was going with her. So we both used the situation and each other to our advantage as most people do. You were on the "watched" list with Linda if you didn't pass the smell test, and Sandy didn't pass. That meant that Linda would be watching her; waiting to be proved right or wrong about her instincts. I honestly got upset with Linda the very first time that she mentioned to me that she had a bad feeling about Sandy. Sandy was the love of my life and my sister would have to accept her, like it or not.

I should have thanked God more often than I did back then. I was quick to blame all bad things on God and his lack of concern for me and slow to thank him when I looked at my wife and my children and all that we had. In fact, I seldom thought of God; we tend to not need him unless we have a problem anyway. My childhood was pretty religious and things had happened that sort of burned me out about the whole religion thing. A priest had knocked me down once for putting water in his wine during a mass. After mass when we were back in the vestibule, Father Carrick had made it very clear that he wanted wine only, "just give the appearance of adding water," he said. My father got so upset about it that after almost killing Father Carrick, he never went back to church at all.

The next glitch in our lives came when Sandy lost her mother to cancer on March 10th, 1978. It was the first taste of loss in either of our immediate families and Sandy and her sisters did not take it well at all. They lost a great deal of respect for their father as they listened to the lessons of life spoken softly by their dying mother. One of the things she told them was that she had spent her whole life with a man she didn't love for the sake of her seven children. And she told them that it was not worth it and to make damn sure that they didn't make the same mistake. To this day, I still remember what she told them, "don't stay with someone you don't love! You only get to live one time and don't waste it like I have." Those words of wisdom from their mother would have a great impact on Sandy and would ultimately affect every one of us and change our lives completely.

The family together in 1980.

CHAPTER TWO:
THE BEGINNING OF THE END

I probably don't really have to tell you what happened soon after they lost their mother. All three of the sisters began having problems. They suffered from depression, had problems with their personal lives at home and in a nutshell, they went through hell. Sandy almost immediately began riding that emotional roller coaster of her own. She started changing; the happy-go-lucky girl I had married began to disappear. Over the next year she became even more moody, would argue over silly things and she began to care less and less about things like our credit and our bills. Our sex life began to suffer too, as if she no longer had any desire for me. We talked less and less, and I was too stupid to even see it. When we did talk about things, she would get touchy and I'd just leave it be rather than get her all wound up.

She began to belittle me even more, even if I had done something right I got no praise from her. She asked me one night if I would mind if she went out with some girlfriends one weekend, she said that she could use some fun away from home. She was not much of a drinker, so this was something new. I told her that I thought it was a good idea and it would do her some good. That Saturday night she met up with some friends and headed out. She must have had a great time because she came home drunk and laughing like a hyena. I do know that we made love that night. It was as if either the alcohol or the evening out had closed the growing distance between us. After that, it became more common for her and her friends to get together and go out. And I was all for it. She seemed happier, and it gave her something to look forward to that she seemed to really enjoy.

Over a period of time, the number of girls going out on these excursions grew and most of the time they would meet at our place. It turned into the best place for them to gather and get ready to go out together. I'm sure you know the secret plan; leave their own homes dressed down as if this was no big deal and then come over to our house where they would get all dolled up and head out for a night of fun. Just like a teen leaving home all nonchalant and as soon as possible putting on her Madonna clothes and makeup.

So that is how it started. Sometimes innocent things lead into something else. This was an innocent beginning, but it sure didn't stay that way for long. Soon these girls were running around our place half-naked as if they were at home. How does any man ignore all of this when he's in a room in his own home and some girl he hardly knows runs in almost naked and says, "don't mind me, I just need to iron this," and then goes about it as if he is not there. All of this happened over a period of time. And over that period of time, innocent things became blatant advances. It really was a small beginning that led to a lot of problems. All of these girls quickly got comfortable at our house. Our place was where they could go from a group who could be Girl Scout leaders or women who were going out to bingo, to a bunch of girls that looked like hookers when they left, all dolled up and ready for anything.

Before long, some of the girls were teasing me, and I started teasing them back. One would stick her head in the room and say, "don't look, I have to get something and I'm not dressed." It sometimes turned into playful threats of blackmail such as: "I'm going to tell Sandy about that look on your face when I bent over," or, "do you like what you see? I'd rather just stay here with you and let them all go out." You know exactly what I mean, the inevitable things that can and will happen. Some would do things on purpose to get me excited, like pull their panties down halfway and smile and put a finger to their mouth as if to say, "Don't tell Sandy." Over time, some would come into the living room and kiss me or bend over right in front of me waiting for me to touch them while the others were in another room getting dressed. Sounds crazy, but it was hell! And it was a hell of a thrill, too. It became hell on earth to not touch, or to turn away. Exactly what would you have done? Pretty depressing when I think back now though. Is it a wonder that Sandy was not the only one that looked forward to the weekend? I was giving Sandy as much money as I could so that they wouldn't cancel the weekend girls' thing; hell, I was giving money to the others who said they couldn't afford to go out so that they would! We were falling into a big hole and I didn't want to stop it.

Sandy knew that our sex life was falling apart, and a few of the girls were beginning to tell me that Sandy had a secret. But at the time I was too damn busy thinking about all the half-naked girls running around our house to care. I certainly didn't want it to stop; it was a new and exciting thrill every time they got together.

A few of the girls would tell me that Sandy was seeing someone else. I would ask her about it and she'd tell me that it wasn't true. I was giving her space, because she needed some. All of this led up to more and more. On one occasion one of them came over on a very cold night in the middle of the week, an extremely rare thing. I was confused by her arrival as she came in the door, and I told her that Sandy had just left for Ashtabula to meet her at a shopping mall and she said, "I know, I'll be a little late, car trouble." Then she asked if the kids were asleep, and when I said yes, she slid her jeans off and threw them at me. I became weak, giving in to whatever form of loving or sympathy I could get. Sometimes they would call to tell me that Sandy had said that she was going to meet someone later. By this time, I was sleeping with more than one of them and I thought that they were testing me to see if I would care enough to throw Sandy out and move them in. It's funny how cloudy a man thinks when another woman is pulling his zipper down.

All of this was kept out of the eyes of the kids at all times. They saw nothing and knew nothing. No matter how bad things were getting, their mother and I always put the kids first. I know, it sounds like bullshit, but it's true. All of the crazy things that were going on did not affect the kids. Life was as normal as normal can be for them; stories at bedtime, playing games on the living room floor, making snowmen out in the yard in the winter, all the things that families do together, we did.

Anyway, I never knew what was going to happen on any given night, and frankly, it was pretty exciting. I was always wound up while the girls were out because there was always the chance that Sandy would come home and want to reach out for me. I'd take it, even if it was the alcohol. Sometimes I would be awakened by Sandy and another girl, both tearing their clothes off and both crawling into our bed.

I began to hear things from others, people that knew us but didn't know about our problems; people that were not a part of the crazy things but were old friends and neighbors. Close friends would tell me that Sandy was seen a few times with some guy at one of the clubs in town. Sandy would say that it was just friendly chatter with someone who had bought her a drink, or it was an old friend, or it was someone she had gone to school with. I always gave her the benefit of the doubt, although I knew better. But she had changed; she wasn't the person I had married. And as a matter of fact, I had changed too. Our marriage was simply one of convenience by now. It was just more convenient to stay together than it was to go through all the splitting up bullshit. So even though things had changed, we were together, although it was now much different than before. Have you ever worked all day and had that desire so strong inside you to be home that you just couldn't wait to get there and be with the person you love? Well, I had that feeling for a long time and now that feeling was gone. I'm lucky; at least I know what that feeling was like. Most people will probably never know the feeling I'm talking about. I had it and lost it.

She was not the same. Her temper was shorter; her levels of patience and tolerance were plummeting. In general, nothing really mattered to her anymore except the kids. She stopped worrying about money like she always had; now it was if you want it, buy it; if you can't afford it, get it anyway. What the hell, you only live once. Her sisters both went through divorces and it had become a throwaway world for all of them. I was not the same either. We still did things together as a family, but other than that, we had no normal sex life and pretty much no relationship. The girls' night out stuff had finally come to an end; it had run its course and now couldn't satisfy her, and besides, the ramifications of all that bullshit were really affecting a lot of people. Good people.

Sandy and I bought her mother's house later that year. It wasn't much, but it would be ours, and maybe it would settle us down. It was a one-bedroom house with a cubbyhole space near the bathroom door, just enough room for bunk beds for the two kids. Many a night I sat there and read stories to them as they lay in their bunks, crammed into too small of a space and stuck next to the water heater. If you opened the bathroom door too far it would hit the bunk bed, that's how small of a bedroom the kids had. But there was never a complaint from either of them.

She was seeing someone behind my back. I knew it. I was told about it by friends I trusted. I didn't want to believe it. She was very confused and always reliving what her mother had said about settling for something rather than living the one life you get. Her sisters and friends were not helping much either, because they were going through the same things as she was. About mid-1980 sometime, I learned that Sandy had been asking my father for money. She was going to him and telling him that we had bills we could not pay and that the kids were doing without something or other, and that I was too proud to go to him. We didn't have it easy, but we were making it without any help. I never saw the money she was getting from Dad; what she was doing with it I still don't know. My father never mentioned anything about it to me. He either fell for her story hook, line and sinker, or he just felt that it wasn't worth discussing with me. Either way, I was oblivious to the situation and therefore unable to put a stop to it. And looking back now that my father has passed away, it makes me wonder just what he thought of me back then. Was he disappointed in me?

There was never a time that I did not work. I have been working since I was 13 years old. I, like my older brother Alan, began working at the Ford dealership where our father worked; both of us started when we became 13. My responsibilities included going up and down each row of cars and washing every one, every day after school. It made no difference if it was raining or snowing, we did it anyway. And like Alan before me, father would have our checks made out to him, and then pay us in cash, exactly half of what we had earned each week. "Room and board," he would say when you questioned him, "lessons in life." And it was also our responsibility to get there, however we could. It was about 15 miles from our home, so this was always a problem. I distinctly remember one very cold afternoon where Alan and I had to walk about four miles to get there in the snow and stiff wind, and I would never have made it without his constant pushing me to keep up with him. We froze our asses off that time, but we got there, bloody noses and frozen fingers and all. Dad withheld one half of my paycheck every week of every year until the time came that I quit and went to work at the truck stop where Sandy and I had met. And now we are back to the check that my father gave me at my wedding reception, and now you understand just how bad I felt at that very moment when I had opened that card. I felt bad for all of the fun and laughter that dad and I missed out on because I was mad at him all those years for keeping half of my money. The minute I read the note inside the card at our reception, I understood why he did it. And I was ashamed of myself.

I was a lot of things as a younger man, but I was very proud that I had and always would, provide for my family. I was raised that way. My father was a great influence on me and I will be forever grateful for that. He was one of the greatest people I have ever known, and when we lost him, the world truly lost one of the biggest hearted people that ever lived. My father was a big man. And with that big man came a huge heart, one that had room for everyone he ever met.

Dad was the oldest of seven kids and he quit school in the eighth grade so that he could work to help support his brothers and sisters. My grandfather was an alcoholic who worked in a factory that made crankshafts for big trucks. Each payday, grandpa would get drunk and spend a large portion of his paycheck on booze, then wind up going home drunk. My father, being the oldest, would put his father in the bathtub and let him puke and piss on himself until he slept himself sober. That is why Dad had to quit school, to help his mother raise and support the family. My father acquired a strong sense of responsibility to provide for others; to provide first for his brothers and sisters and mother, and later in life to provide for his wife and seven children. That is why Dad dealt us kids the discipline that he did: he hoped the life lessons that he had learned the hard way would make us better people. It was also the reason why my father never drank, and probably the reason why I didn't drink much either. And he didn't stop there, he continued to help others his whole life, until finally, his health failing, he slipped away to the Lord and the open arms that surely awaited him.

My father had worked his way up from a used car salesman to General Manager of the largest Ford dealership in the area, Ferraro Ford. But after suffering a couple of heart attacks, he gave them his keys back and told them where they could stick them and he opened his own used car lot, a small lot where he catered to lower income people. Dad was known in the area for his big heart and he had helped more people in his lifetime than anyone could count.

The nicest thing that I ever heard said about my father came from a complete stranger at my father's funeral. I was standing alone in front of his casket thanking him for all the times he guided, directed, spanked, yelled at, and rescued me. This man walked up alongside of me, asked if I was one of his sons and after I acknowledged that I was, proceeded to tell me an amazing story about how my father had helped him and his family, yet never wanted to admit that he had. That was Dad, without a doubt. He never enjoyed the limelight, choosing rather to silently savor the thought that someone's life was now better.

As this man spoke, I couldn't help but begin to cry, and as his words came they described my father and his modus operandi to a tee. The man smiled as he told me about how he had fallen into a well on his farm, breaking both legs. He was behind on payments, his farm in jeopardy. One day he was at the local bank (West Springfield branch of the Albion Bank), pleading with a loan officer either for more time, or for money to carry him through until he could work his farm again. For whatever reason, he was told they could not help him. He said that he had no hope left as he rolled his wheelchair out the door and asked the Lord for help, as all other options were gone.

The man said that the next day the bank notified him that $5,000 had been deposited into his account. As any of us would have, he asked in bewilderment how that could be, and he was told the depositor specifically wanted to remain anonymous. The man told me about how this selfless gift had salvaged his farm and his belief in humanity. He said that he relived that visit to the bank over and over in his mind for years and thought about who it could have been that had helped him and who may have been in the bank that day. Finally, he remembered seeing my father in line.

As we both stood in front of my Dad's casket, he said that when he realized it had to have been my father that had helped him, he went to find him and confirm it. He found Dad at his used car lot, the same place where I had witnessed my father help countless people. He said he told my father straight out that he needed to say thanks, to let him know just how much his help had meant to him and his family. He told me Dad had smiled and said, "I don't know who it was that helped you, but it wasn't me." The man said the look of satisfaction on my father's face gave it all away and after a while and as they chatted, he confessed, asking that it not be brought up ever again. And according to the man, it never was until he told me.

Time went on and as it did, my relationship with Sandy got colder than the winter weather outside. We were cordial to each other and still slept together, although sex was rare and generally happened only when she felt guilty about something.

Brian and Melissa were growing up happy and healthy and completely unaware that problems existed. When we did anything as a family we put on a good facade. I don't think anyone within our families knew that we were struggling to keep our marriage together. Most of Sandy's friends were going through divorces or already divorced by this time and were always bragging to her about how you can have your cake and eat it too, if you do things the right way. They seemed to be rubbing it in to her about the freedom and control they had now that they had separated from their husbands; money when you need it, a sitter when you need that, and control of everything. And after you get the house and car you get the child support money every month. I look back now and see all these things clearly and wish they had been a little clearer back then.

My father and I had opened a small body shop about this time, Schulz's Auto Body, in West Springfield, Pennsylvania. Dad had the used car lot up the street at the intersection of Routes 20 and 5, and I ran the body shop and acted as manager, body man, estimator and painter. At first, I did all of Dad's used cars, but as time went on I got busy enough that Dad's cars became second fiddle to others that paid more. We were actually making money! Dad was getting his cars done inexpensively, and I was drawing a decent paycheck and all the bills were getting paid. I did exactly what I had always done, get up early, go to work, work hard and go home feeling good about putting in the kind of day that you can be proud of. But then, I was taught that way. I would go home, play with the kids, have supper and spend time with my family. I loved my family more than anything, and they gave me the very reason to work hard. I did all the things that good dads do, I played with the kids and read them stories, a habit I had acquired from my mother, and I gave them all the love I had. As things fell apart with their mother, the kids and I got closer. My son began the habit of running up to me as I came in the door each night, grabbing me around the legs and wracking me with his head in the process. I would open the door and get hit in the nuts with his head almost every night, and I didn't mind at all. Melissa would run to me too, always wanting picked up and carried by her daddy. Weekends we would do things together, with or without their mother, and as time went on, it was more and more without her.

When I had a complete paint job to do, I would get the car fully ready to spray; sand, wipe down, mask and then tack it off. After that I would rinse down the walls and floor with a garden hose, carefully wetting everything except the car itself so that the dust in the air could settle into the water while I was gone, go home for a while and go back in after the kids were asleep and then paint the car. This was absolutely the best way to get a quality paint job, the kind I could be proud of; the kind that gives you a good reputation. Unfortunately, it left Sandy alone a lot. When the right thing to do was be at home, I was at the shop trying to make a name for myself. All it did was make matters worse.

There was a restaurant in town that became the place to be seen after all the bars closed. This was where everyone seemed to meet after a night of drinking and partying. It was also the best place for coffee in the morning. You could hear all about what had happened in town the night before and who had been seen with whom.

I was not the drinker in our marriage, that's not to say I didn't drink, but I was the one who stayed home so she could go out. I did this for two reasons, the first being that I loved to be home with the kids, as I always was and will be a homebody. The second being that my staying home gave her more freedom and a little freedom can relieve a lot of pressure. After an evening out, one morning Sandy got up and although I had coffee made, she was adamant about going to that particular restaurant for coffee. I was against her going and told her so. She downplayed the importance of going as if it was no big deal and then went anyway, knowing I was upset about it. As usual, Sandy did what Sandy wanted to do. It pissed me off and gave me the feeling that something was going on, so I immediately called a friend and asked if I could drop the kids off for a few minutes while I did something important.

After doing so, I went to the restaurant and saw Sandy sitting with some people I didn't know. There was a woman and two guys sitting with her. The looks on their faces were of surprise mixed with a little guilt, as if they were up to something and wondering if they had been caught, or as if Glen knew something was up, but just how much did he know and what the hell was he going to do? Sandy stood up quickly, said hi and then began to introduce me to the others; friends she had met while out one night, she said. There was a couple that I will call Jack and Jill, and Ralph, a friend of theirs in town from out of state. They offered me a seat and a cup of coffee, but the situation was very uncomfortable for me so I simply asked Sandy when she thought she would be home so we could talk and I left.

I was pissed. I knew something was up, and I suspected that Ralph was the one Sandy had been seen with, but I did not know for sure. Maybe I was just jumping to conclusions, I thought. It didn't take long for Sandy to come home and start explaining the whole situation away as if they were practically family. She made it sound like they were the nicest people on earth and I needed to get to know them before I jumped to conclusions. Yeah, right. I passed judgment on them as soon as I met them and it has never changed. But I listened. Jack was an out-of-work mechanic, a (pardon the pun) jack of all trades guy with health problems brought on by years of self-abuse, and his wife, Jill, was the breadwinner of the two (that always tells me something). They had no children, so the loves of their lives were their Harleys. The other guy was Ralph, a friend of theirs who was in town on his Harley for a visit. I remember noticing that his hair was longer than any of the women around us. Rumor had it that he was unemployed as well. Gee, I wonder why. Over time I came to accept that these people were her friends and that if I wanted to stay with my wife, I would have to tolerate them at least until they, as everything else with Sandy, got old. I learned to be reluctantly polite when our paths crossed.

I was doing pretty well at the body shop. I was painting cars, boats and even started painting motorcycles. Money is money. I had begun to build a reputation in the area and people were coming in; coming in all day long! I was getting so busy that I couldn't get any work done. And over time I began to spend more and more time at work, and less and less at home. And when I was home, I focused on the kids. We would play in the yard, play with Midnight, our dog, or read together.

Sandy and I were so far apart that the fact we still lived together and even slept together was amazing. We had learned to live with each other without discussing our problems and without any love life whatsoever. The love given and shared with the kids became enough, and it was constant and never wavered, not once; the kids were the only thing we could always agree on. I believe that we had the appearance of a happy family to anyone looking and our relationship was never violent, I was never the violent kind. What I didn't know was that my family could see signs of trouble and yet they said nothing to me. I thought I was hiding and covering things so well that no one would see anything. I also didn't know that Sandy was still asking my father for money behind my back. She had promised to tell me if we were in a money crunch so that I could figure out how to get us out of it and I knew we were doing okay. I realize now that she was taking advantage of a good thing and saving up money on the side. She was also taking part-time jobs and putting money away, or if not, she was spending more and more without my knowledge. She would go to Dad every so often and tell him we needed something and couldn't afford it, and Dad would always give her money and not say a word to me; probably thinking I would be hurt or ashamed, when in truth I would have known what was really happening. She was up to something, saving money for some reason. She had a plan, and I was soon to find out what it was.

CHAPTER THREE:
FINDING GOD THE HARD WAY

I will always remember this day vividly; I had a complete paint job on a black van and I had prepared the van, swept the floor and positioned the van in the middle of the shop away from any wall to make sure no dirt, spider webs or trash could contaminate my paint job. I had watered down the walls and floor to contain dust like I always did. All was ready, just let any stirred up dust settle, tack off the van with a tack rag (a cloth with beeswax on it to capture any dirt) and shoot it. I went home, no better place to be to kill time while the dust settled onto the wet floor. I walked in the door and was grabbed around the legs and wracked, as usual. My son really missed me and loved hugging me by the legs when he first saw me, painful as it sometimes was, it was a good feeling. I spent some time with the kids and we put them to bed, Sandy and I both. I then kissed her and told her I would see her later, I had to go spray the van and would be back in about three hours.

It was probably about midnight when I pulled into the driveway and I saw Sandy come out the side door and sit on the steps. As I walked up to her I asked her why she was still up. That's when I saw the suitcase. I wondered what was going on, my fatigued brain taking its sweet time correlating data. Where the hell would she be going? Why only one suitcase? If she were moving out, she would need several suitcases. Maybe someone needs her, something must have happened to someone in her family. "Don't go in the house!" I heard it, but it didn't compute. "What?" I asked. Then I heard it again, "Don't go in the house. You don't live here anymore, and I have someone here with me," and she pointed through a window to a man inside my house, sitting on my couch. I could see that it was Ralph, Jack and Jill's friend. "Are you serious?" I remember saying, as if stuck in some kind of time warp. It was as if she had pushed a pause button on time itself. I honestly thought that it was some stupid joke that was being played on me.

"I packed you a suitcase until I can box up all your things," her voice quivered as she spoke. She was taking lots of deep breaths. Now some people will think that I'm nutless because I didn't rip the door off, go in and throw the prick out or strangle him and then punch her on the way out. But anyone who knows me would tell you that that's not me; and that's not what I did. I stood there thinking about how pitiful she looked. For the first time in my life, I could see how unhappy she was, and I realized how much her mother's death had fucked her up. She was scared, shaking, waiting, undoubtedly worried about my next move. Without saying another word, I picked up the suitcase and left.

I drove a few miles down the road, pulled over and wondered what the hell had just happened. I didn't want to believe that I had just been thrown out of my home. I thought that I should go right back there, grab the two kids and tell Sandy and dickhead to have a nice life. We would still be a family; just a family without her. I thought about a lot of things, such as maybe I should go back and kill the bastard. It was probably all his fault anyway, Sandy was probably innocent, just confused. I drove and drove and eventually realized I had nowhere to go to, so I decided to check into the nearest motel, the Hollywood Motel in Kingsville, Ohio. Even with a blurred mind at the time, I remember seeing letters tattooed onto the knuckles of the girl that checked me in that night, the letters from both hands adding up to say "fuck you." I knew then that I was at the right place, it just fit. I checked in, sat on the bed and surveyed my place in life, all night. It was a long night.

I wound up thinking that she was confused, and in a few days, she would find me and say she was sorry and that she wanted me to come home. Yes, no doubt about it. She'd get laid, feel guilty as hell, find me, tell me she was sorry, and ask me to come home! And then she would be better than ever, she'd have all of this out of her system. She would probably turn into a nymphomaniac trying to appease me. It would work out just fine in the end; I was sure of it, after all, I loved her. It was the best thought I could keep at the time. With that thought came a feeling that almost made me smile, I could sleep some.

After the first two days I was watching the door anywhere I happened to be, always looking to see if it was Sandy who was coming in. I was sure sooner or later she would come. I jumped every time a phone rang; again thinking that it was Sandy calling to tell me to come home. Sleep is hard to find at times like that. You spend a lot of time reliving your life and your part in whatever mess you have on your hands. You begin to soul search. You feel pain, as big a pain as you have ever felt. You realize that now you know what it's like to be tossed aside. It takes you back in time as you wonder if you ever inflicted the same pain on someone else unknowingly, or worse, uncaringly. And you feel worthless. I likened myself to a used sanitary pad.

One morning I woke up in my shitty little room, grabbed the electric water heater wand my mother had just given me, plugged it into the outlet, stuck it in my coffee cup full of cold water and instant coffee, and patiently waited. As it warmed the water and the crap in the cup began to resemble coffee, I was hit by the greatest pain I had ever felt. It was an overwhelming sense of loss, the loss of my children. I realized then that I could live without Sandy, but life without the kids would be beyond my ability to survive. I cried like a baby. The one thing I failed to do at that time was ask God for help. I felt that he had turned his back to me.

Later that day I broke down and did what I told myself early on never to do; I called Sandy. I asked if I could please come home. She said no. I asked how the children were. I asked how she was. I asked her if she needed money or anything else. I asked anything I could think of, anything to keep her on the phone and keep the possibility alive, the possibility that I could talk her into letting me come home.

She told me that she had gotten her first tattoo. She said that she would show me the next time she saw me. Neither one of us had ever wanted a tattoo before. I was a little shocked, but pretended it was nice, the "I'm happy for you" shit you say when you're groveling and kissing ass. Then she made it clear that I was bothering her. She told me that she was tired of being a wife, tired of being a mother and tired of never getting a chance to be just herself. "I just want to be me for a while," she said. She was short, to the point, and cold, terribly cold. It was horrible. And I was miserable; hell, I wished I had never called her at all. I felt worse, I felt worthless, and I felt like life wasn't worth living. I was a pile of shit in a toilet and no one had enough mercy to hit the handle and send me away.

The next morning I drove over to my mother's house and in a sense said goodbye without actually saying it. My mother was the greatest of them all. I will never forget what she gave up for us kids and the life she gave up for my father. She sailed away from her family, her country and her way of life for him.

I talked to Mom at great length that day, although I probably did nothing except ramble and whine about all my problems. But Mom listened intently the whole time, obviously worried about me and the kids. She had no way to help, but if she could have, she would have. She also had no way to know what I was going to do later that day and where she would be seeing me next. I didn't either.

After I left mothers, I went to see Doctor Doran, the good doctor we used to live above, because I felt like hammered shit. I told him that Sandy and I had split up and she had a new man and she had both our kids, and that I had nothing to live for. He gave me a prescription for an antidepressant, a drug called Sinequan. When I picked up the prescription, I also bought a bottle of Anacin, a big bottle. I went to the motel and heated up another cup of coffee and sat alone in the darkness, again. You can only take so much loneliness before it eats into you like rust and if the loneliness doesn't get to you the silence will. When I couldn't stand it anymore I left the motel and headed for the nearest bar. Four or five drinks could not ease the pain; the alcohol only making matters worse. The reality of it all was overwhelming. There was a man sitting in my house on my couch watching my television. He was sleeping in my bed, making love to my wife and he was probably either being mean to my children, or being very nice, so nice that they won't want me back either. My children have probably already forgotten who I am. And Sandy just wants a chance to be Sandy. And who cares? No one does. God sure doesn't, or this never would have happened in the first place. To make matters worse, some asshole in the bar went and played a song that ripped my heart out and smashed it, a song called " One" (is the loneliest number you'll ever do), by Three Dog Night. If you know the song, run through the words quickly and you'll understand how helpful it was at the time.

So I said fuck it, enough is enough. I made my way back to my motel room and swallowed the whole bottle of Sinequan. I followed it with the entire bottle of Anacin. It was time I did what a man should do, kiss it all goodbye. The whole fucking world could kiss my ass. I did not leave a note or say any goodbyes. It was late, nearly one a.m. I filled up the car at the nearest gas station, and with a six-pack of beer got on I-90 heading east. I tried to stay at 100 miles per hour as best I could, but I remember that at that speed, it was hard to maneuver around traffic. I never really thought that I might kill someone else; I really didn't want to hurt anyone but myself. I just wanted to drive until I passed out and the car could go off the road and hit whatever it wanted to. If the pills didn't kill me the car accident surely would. Who gave a shit? I watched for the police, too. I figured that if they saw me going that fast they would try to pull me over and that would give me an excuse to go even faster. Between the police and the pills or the passing out and crashing into something, any way you looked at it, I was going to die that night. I didn't really care how.

I had passed from Ohio into Pennsylvania and gone probably 50 miles or so and had finished off the beer when I heard a few more songs that confirmed that I needed to die, like "Dust in the Wind," by Kansas, and I started feeling awful, my body starting to react to the medicine and alcohol mix, and I began to feel an immediate sensation each time my body absorbed more of the drugs, sort of like a series of shots in a row, each more powerful than the previous one and less than a minute apart. I realized I had not seen a police car anywhere. Go figure. I was always mindful of the police and normally kept within the law to avoid them. That night I wanted them to find me and push me off the highway, and they were nowhere to be found, probably sitting somewhere eating donuts. I was getting violently sick now, and I began to vomit on myself. My sight became blurred, but I didn't mind at all. I thought dying would be more painful than this, this wasn't so bad, I thought. It looked like this would be a piece of cake; just a little more pain and it would be over. My mindset was the same, no one cared if I died or not. Funny how greedy you can be when you can't think straight. I took a strange pleasure in pissing my pants as I drove, not a time to worry about the small things, I thought. I rolled down the window and threw my wallet out, thinking that I wouldn't be needing it where I was going. Besides, when they found me I didn't want them to know who I was, just bury me. Mark me as unknown male number whatever; in plot number who gives a shit. The hell with it. The whole damn thing was humiliating anyhow and I'd rather be unknown.

Things were getting worse by the minute, and yet time seemed like it was standing still. The six-pack was long gone by now and I was puking a lot but trying to swallow and keep it down. I needed more beer just to keep from vomiting, I thought. I was losing consciousness now too, and each time my body absorbed more of the drugs, it tried its best to reject it and keep me alive.

I started to lose the ability to keep the car on the road. I had passed through Pennsylvania and was now in New York. I was feeling the absolute worst I had ever felt in my entire life, puking my guts out all over myself, sweating profusely, urine soaked, and crying. And then, all of a sudden out of nowhere, God spoke to me. He really did. He asked me to think about Brian and Melissa. He asked me how I thought my parents would take the news of my death. God told me that even if I thought that the kids didn't need me right now, they would need me later on in life. And what kind of a piece of shit father would take himself out of the lives of his kids because *HE* is not happy? Maybe there is a reason I should live, I thought. I was always a responsible person, and my responsibility is to help make good adults of my children. My responsibilities included being there for them. Life would surely suck, but I needed to live and I needed to be there for the kids if they ever needed me. Responsibility is a heavy burden to bear and bearing it was how we were raised.

I can remember looking down at my lap and seeing a hell of a mess all the way down to my shoes, and I felt like death wasn't too far away. I really think I was at the edge. I struggled to let go of the hurting that put me in this position. I knew then that I had to live, and that I had reasons to live, two of them, ages seven and five, but taking corrective actions at this point was out of my control. I had a full-blown conversation with the Lord. I told him how sorry and ashamed I was and how grateful I would be if he would listen to me for just a minute and help me; help me right now, please Lord. I told him that I was sorry for not thinking about him sooner and sorry for not thanking him for anything he may have helped me with in the past. I also told him how sorry I was for thinking only of myself and not about my children or my parents or anyone else that cared about me.

I was crying as I drove, my stomach causing me to wretch in pain. I must have said the words "please God, please help me right now," at least 25 times in a row. I tried to keep looking in front of me but could barely keep my head up. I desperately tried to focus long enough to see an exit, and if put there on purpose, there it was. I had no idea where I was. I remember seeing it and slamming on the brakes and skidding, and I remember how happy it made me feel that I made it. I took the exit and I followed it as it made a left turn up over the freeway and into complete darkness. I was in the middle of nowhere. I don't remember seeing anything, not even a streetlight anywhere. I was between a rock and a hard place because I couldn't stay conscious long enough to think. I just kept going, and then I saw the side of a brick building, a big brick building. I remember smiling and saying, "Thank you, Lord."

I pointed the car at the side of the building and that was that.

I woke up in the emergency room and there were people all around me. They were yelling at me, talking to me relentlessly. My head hurt; hell, all of me hurt, and the yelling wasn't helping at all. "What did you take? Tell us what you took," over and over, I heard them saying, all of it just pissing me off. All that yelling was making my head hurt so badly that I thought they were trying to kill me. I was out of my mind at the time anyway, not really knowing what was going on. Just be quiet, I thought, please be quiet. They were pumping my stomach, that and the way my body was fighting off all the drugs I had swallowed made me wish I had died. They kept after me, asking what I had taken, asking me what my name was. After awhile I started to understand what was happening, and I realized that I was still alive, and that made me feel a little better. It also made me feel completely humiliated. If I had ever been ashamed of myself, it was now. I told them that I had swallowed over a hundred pills, a mixture of Sinequan, Anacin and an awful lot of alcohol, too. I wanted to help them help me, I wanted to live, but I was just too ashamed and too sick to tell them my name or why I did this. Now they were making me drink some charcoal milkshake kind of shit, and I was gagging like hell. I was convulsing from all the crap my body had absorbed and I again wanted to be dead.

I started opening and closing my eyes as I was coming to later, and I began to hear familiar voices. It seemed like it took forever before I realized that my parents were there, each holding one of my hands. My mother smiled as she said, "Hi." My father told me that I was going to be all right. They told me that I was out for almost two days before I opened my eyes. God, I'm sorry I put them through that. There aren't many things in my life I would change if I could, but that's one of them. Not because of the pain I felt, but because of the pain they felt. It was the stupidest thing I have ever done, and looking back, I can't believe I almost left my children without their father.

As it turned out, a woman working as a paramedic had recognized me and called my parents. The woman was the daughter of one of my father's best friends, a man we grew up calling Uncle Leroy. He wasn't really our uncle, but we knew him as that all of our lives. This was his oldest daughter, Lisa. She just happened to wind up there that particular night. Lisa is now a doctor. What a small world it is. Lisa, I'm sorry that you had to be the one to call my parents.

Dad told me that the car was a total loss. He said I had imbedded it into the side of a small town fire station and finding it probably saved my life. I didn't find it at all, it was the Lord that found it and it was the Lord that saved my life that night. How else can you explain my finding the only place in a completely unknown area that could possibly help me? Thank you, Lord, I will thank you every day for the rest of my life.

CHAPTER FOUR:
ACCEPTING REALITY

They don't release you after you have attempted suicide, they put you in a mental health unit for a while to determine your sanity. I was moved back to Erie and put in a local hospital. It's one of those places where you are locked in and there are no sharp objects anywhere. The room wasn't bad, similar to a small hotel room except that it had been designed to safely secure someone who wanted to take themselves out; I already had that chance and chose to live. The next morning they brought me to an office where I was introduced to a female doctor. I don't know whether she was a psychiatrist or a psychologist, I couldn't tell you the difference anyhow. I can tell you she was very calm and direct in her questioning. "What caused you to do what you did?" she asked. "I miss my kids and I don't think I can live without them," I told her. "Where are your children and why are you separated from them?" she asked next. I explained the whole story to her. My wife of almost 10 years threw me away like an old shoe and to make it even worse, she replaced me before a cold spot could form in our bed. I told her that I fell apart like a cardboard box left out in the rain. I told her that I realized my marriage was over and that I needed to be around for whenever I got the chance to see my kids. I saw her for about 30 to 45 minutes each day over a period of about three days, I guess. Each time I spoke with her I told her how stupid I felt for even thinking about suicide, and that my only concern was for Brian and Melissa. She said that she would talk to Sandy and see what she could do to help. She asked me about my thoughts on suicide in general, and I explained that I knew according to my religion that suicide would prevent me from ever going to heaven and I explained that having already had the opportunity to do so, I chose to live and I had no intentions of ever attempting it again.

They told me one morning that Sandy was coming to see me that day. It pleased me greatly. It put me right back to square one in my hopes of reconciliation. She was going to talk to the shrink and the shrink would tell her just how much I loved her and all would be better. Then she would tell me how sorry she was for starting this mess in the first place and how badly she felt. I knew she would say, "When they let you out of here, we're going to start over. You're coming home." I knew she would have good news for me. This mess, this nightmare from hell, would be over, and life would be even better than it was before. From now on I would really appreciate what I had. I counted the minutes. I was beside myself with anxiety. In just a little while this whole shitty mess would be over and it would be the end of the worst nightmare a person could live through. But I did live through, and I would be the better husband and the better father for it. Thank God, she was here.

Yeah, right! What she did was scream at me for damn near leaving the kids without their father. She was right of course, but there was no mercy, no pity, no "It's all my fault." She made it clear that life as I had known it was over and I had better get used to it. She also told me that she had hired an attorney and that she had filed for divorce and custody. She minced no words while berating me for every problem she had, for every problem the two kids would ever have in their entire life and for every problem I had. She rambled about bills and how she would have no choice but to go to my father for help, since I was currently earning no income at all. I asked her about dickweed and whether he was earning a living yet. "He is making some money playing in a country and western band when he can, and his name is Ralph, not dickweed," she said. As she abruptly ended our chat, she said that she was great and Brian and Melissa were just fine. And then she got up and walked away.

While confined in that place, I noticed an old man that would come out of his room and sit on a bench in a hallway each day, and he would sit there all day long. He would say nothing, just sit there and wait for time to pass. I went over and sat on the bench with him one afternoon. He said not a word unless spoken to by the staff. I didn't either, I just sat there with him for several hours one day, and then I got up and walked away.

The next morning I went over and sat with him again, and this time I spoke up. I asked him what his name was and I told him mine. I told him why I was there and all that and when he didn't offer his story, I asked him. He said that his wife had passed away last year and that he had no children. He had no living family members either. He did not want to live but said that he was either too healthy or too stubborn to die. That night, Mary secretly allowed me a pen and paper and I wrote this poem. I called it simply,

"Ode of the Elderly"

Too old to work, too young to die, goddamn, I'm starting to cry.
My wife? Last year she passed away; what the hell can I do today?
My son has grown up; he has sons of his own.
Next week he'll be moving, he bought a new home.
Yes my son will be moving to far, far away
and I'll be so lonely, but well, it's okay.
My life has been good and the Lord has been kind,
soon it will end and I really won't mind.

Yes I'm old and I'm gray and I'll add if I may, do you care?
Will you help? Then come see me someday.

Copyright © 1981

One of the people that worked in the mental health unit
was a girl named Mary Conti. Of the few good memories that
I have about the place, she's one of them and I remember her
and how she was so kind to me, always treating me like a fellow human being, not some basket case. She would explain to
me why she was doing whatever she was doing. For example,
she would check my room before I could go in, just in case
some other nutcase had done something or placed something
in the room. She had to hand me a razor and then watch me
shave in case I tried something crazy. She became a friend after
she found out why I had done what I had, and she knew inside
that I didn't need to be there. She would stare at me and then
tell me I didn't belong there, "I was an anomaly," she said. I
wish I could remember all of the things she did for me, like
telling me who to avoid because they were nuts or dangerous;
or to watch out for that girl because she would steal anything
she could. Mary would sneak me into the cafeteria after hours
and we would have a cigarette and coffee together and talk.
She talked to me like a friend and she reassured me that one
day the kids and I would be together and happy. Thank you,
Mary Conti, wherever you are. I'm sure you don't remember
me, but I will always remember you, and you need to know
that you were right. You have no idea how much of an impact
you had on me. You did more for me than any doctor could
have. Your patience, calmness, kindness and logic were much
appreciated and never forgotten.

I think I was in that place for about five days. They realized that part of my depression was that I missed the life I had

had, but more than that, I missed the kids. The shrink told me that the only thing wrong with me was a broken heart and she couldn't help me with that. She had spoken to Sandy and Sandy had made it clear that it was over. Sandy had told her that the marriage was a bad one and that she was not going to look back. The only thing the shrink could do was help me try to accept the fact that it was over.

Mary told me one evening that she had seen Sandy there and had quickly determined that I was too damn good for her anyway. She said that if there was one thing she had become good at while doing her job, it was learning how to judge people. She said that I would rise above it all and be the better for it. The last time we saw each other she gave me a quarter in a tiny manila envelope that had her initials on it and as she handed it to me she said to use it to call someone if I ever felt that lonely again. I said goodbye and left. I still have the little envelope and its quarter.

I stayed with my parents for awhile after my release from the hospital. And I immediately went back to working the body shop, trying hard to immerse myself and keep my mind occupied. But my spirit was not really in it and all my ambition was gone. After all the things that had happened, I still had nothing on my mind other than going home and being with the woman I loved and being with my children. It was all I thought about, all I dreamed about and all I wanted. Have you ever wanted something so badly that it was your only reason to live? I would spend eight hours thinking of a reason to call Sandy, just so I could hear her voice, hoping she might say, "Okay, come on home, it's all a big mistake." Of course, she never did. She was always downright nasty, as if making sure that it hurt. It was always short and sweet, "it's over, get over it asswipe, I'll call you if I need anything, don't call me!"

It was now early June of 1981, and my father and I decided

to close the body shop. I was as lost as a man can get. I had only two things on my mind at any given time, I needed my kids, and I wanted to end this nightmare and go home. I thought about doing just that, just walk in, sit down and say "I live here and I'm not leaving. If you're not happy, then get the fuck out of my house."

I would drive past the house again and again, hoping to spot the kids and just see them, just steal a glance and see if they were all right. Sometimes they would be playing in the yard and I would drive slowly by, hoping that they would spot me, hoping that they would give me a sign that they missed me. Most of the time they didn't see me at all and it hurt. The few times that they did see me, one would tell the other and then they would smile and wave or start walking towards the road. I knew that I would have to wave and drive away, I couldn't jeopardize making Sandy any madder. I would drive away waving and smiling, pulling over as soon as I was out of their sight so that I could cry. That hurt even more than not seeing them at all.

I moved out of my parents' house and into the motor home that they kept at the local RV park, Evergreen Lake Park. It was a quiet place surrounding a small lake and it was the place where we had spent many enjoyable days and nights in the past. In fact, it was the place where my son had learned how to ride a bicycle, the perfect place for family get-togethers, picnics and simple pleasures like just relaxing by a fire and cooking marshmallows in the evening.

But it was now a lonely place. I would sit and watch the fire and think about the good times we'd had there, thinking we might never have times like that together again. I could only look forward to the time when Sandy would let me have the kids for awhile. It didn't take long for the loneliness to surface and try to overwhelm me again. I had to occupy myself without being a burden on my family, but that's hard to do when all of your ambition is gone. The arcade game Space Invaders was the big thing at the park at the time and with all the time I had on my hands, I became the park champion on it. The owner of the park would come get me and pay for my play, just so he could watch me and learn from me. He wanted to be as good at it as I was. Most of the time I sat at the camp, alone, listening to songs that seemed to really fit when you're down and out, songs like " Sad Eyes," by Robert John. Songs that make you just want to drink and be miserable. I was miserable, but I did no drinking. It was the drinking that damn near got me killed last time, and drinking never, ever helps.

Sandy began to let me see the children more after a while. I like to think she realized just how important the kids were to me, but the truth was that she enjoyed the time away from them, that freedom that she was seeking. I began to see them a couple of times during the week and at least once on the weekend. Each time I would drive to the house and Sandy would walk them to the car and say goodbye to them. Sometimes she would say take your time, other times she would say be back here in two hours. I never pushed her, I didn't want to screw up the arrangement we had. There would usually be one box of my personal things for me and one bag for the kids each time I went over to pick them up. If Sandy was upset for any reason, the box of my personal things would be nothing but broken pieces of the things that mattered most to me. I had a chess set that my mother had made for me in her ceramics classes. In better times, Sandy and my mother attended the same classes together with Sandy picking up Mom because she never learned how to drive. Sandy went to every class Mom did, and she had told me just how many classes it took mother to make my chess set.

Anyway, the ceramic chess set had been tossed into a box,

one piece at a time, and every piece was either chipped or broken. Mother cried when I showed it to her, not because of the damage, but because of the time spent making the chess pieces, the time she had shared with Sandy. I still have the chess set. Mom tried to fix it but it still shows all the signs of the damage.

I remember a time when Sandy called me at my father's car lot and said she wanted to come and have lunch with me and talk. I got so excited that my father must have thought I was on drugs. I was wound up like a clock, doing what we have all done before, reading more into things than there really was. But hey, there's always a chance, right? This might be it! This could be when she said, "You've paid enough dues, come home." I opened her door for her when she got there, certain now that I must have looked like either a Cheshire cat or a doormat, I'm not sure. I gave her a hug that was received just like a hug you get from someone you never liked, cold and empty. I knew then that it wasn't going to be the kind of meeting I was hoping for. It was then that she realized that she had locked the keys in the car. I guess my running to her door and opening it for her must have caught her off guard. In my haste to be a hero, I damn near destroyed the door trying to get it unlocked for her.

Sandy told me how they were all doing. "She was fine," she said. "The kids were all right, although Brian had been showing a bad attitude and making life difficult for her", she told me. I wasn't sure how to take that, was he interfering with her relationship with Ralph? She said that she was worried about how he would do when school started again, "and Melissa has started crying a lot," she said, "usually about nothing." "Missy," as we called her, "was also becoming a problem to deal with, she would go from just fine to miserably sad without notice." And she made it clear that it was my fault, all of this whole mess was my fault.

She wanted to know what my plans were. She wanted to know how it felt to hurt as bad as I was hurting. How was I going to move on with my life? What was I going to do for a living? Where was I going to live? What did I need from the house? She severed all ties. She let me know that it was really over, like it or not; it was over and I needed to make plans. She wasn't cruel, just matter-of-fact. She spoke as if she was talking about a car that we'd had for a long time, and now it was time to scrap it.

I asked her what she wanted if indeed we divorced and I guess I caught her off guard, because she paused and gave me a funny look. Evidently she hadn't thought about the reality of that question. She got upset with me. "I want the house, I want the car, and I'll take your damn motorcycle and sell it," she said. "We're gonna need the money anyway and you don't really need it. I think it was stupid of you to buy it in the first place."

I told her that I only wanted one thing, the kids. "You let me have the kids and you can have everything else. They are not fitting into your life right now, anyhow," I said. "You just told me Brian was being belligerent on a daily basis." Sandy said, "We'll see."

The last thing she said did startle me though; she asked if I wanted to come to the house Saturday night. She said that she was going to be out most of the night and didn't have a sitter and she thought we could kill two birds with one stone if I spent the evening at the house with the kids. I asked her if I could keep them overnight at Evergreen and she said no, she felt that wouldn't be a good idea. I said yes, of course, still thinking that anything to get me into the picture again, anything at all was better than nothing.

It was strange walking into my own home, a place where I was not welcome and yet the only place I wanted to be! I immediately felt uncomfortable, like a new sitter going to a home for the first time. I was relinquishing all pride, any manliness I had left and all self-respect by being there under those circumstances. But having the kids hanging all over me and seeing them so happy offset the shitty feeling I had, the feeling that I was dirt that had been tracked in by someone else. The whole situation was surreal and improved only after Sandy left. The kids and I had a great time that night. We played and read books and talked about what they had been doing, how they felt, and what thoughts made them feel happy. I could not resist asking some questions that were painful. I asked them if they missed me and how they liked Ralph. I hated asking, but it was necessary, and some of the answers made me feel like shit, but I had to know, I had to find out as much as I could while I had the chance. The kids told me all kinds of things that night.

They told me that sometimes they were being sent outside at night, told to go out in the yard and play for a while. They said that they would get scared and cry and that they didn't like it. I honestly didn't believe them; no one would do that, especially not Sandy. But I told them that if it ever happened again, to go next door to the Seiberts and ask if they could go inside, and they said that they would.

They also told me that sometimes Sandy and Ralph would close the door to the bedroom and leave them alone in the house, telling them to behave and be quiet. They said that almost every night they were being taken to a different house because their mother went out a lot. They told me more than I could absorb at one time, enough to enrage me, and the rage began to overcome the sense of loss that I had been feeling for her. I wound up thinking that she was not the Sandy I could love anymore, after all. I thanked the Lord for being able to spend the time with my children and I fell asleep on the couch after Brian and Melissa nodded off. I had read to them until they couldn't keep their eyes open any longer. My being there had meant a lot to them and it had meant a lot to me as well. I know that they slept well that night. They slept and I began to heal.

About four in the morning I heard the door open. I pretended to be asleep, and I overheard Sandy and another woman talking. I recognized the voice as one of Sandy's friends; I'll call her Carrie. I heard Sandy say something about how pitiful I was and I heard Carrie say something about letting me sleep rather than waking me up and making me leave since Ralph was out of town anyway. I fell back asleep again after it got quiet. Sometime later I was awakened by Carrie, one hand shaking me while she covered my mouth with the other. She whispered to me to be quiet as she took her robe off. She said that she had just made love to Sandy and felt sorry for me and that now it was my turn. She said I deserved it. I couldn't have agreed more.

I began to see things differently after that night. I accepted the reality of things and I began to get on with life. I was still living at the park. It was quiet, inexpensive and there was always someone around to talk to. I went over to see my old boss, George Laituri, and he offered me a job again, so I took him up on it. Although George was battling cancer at the time, he really cared about my problems and he listened intently as I told him about the whole mess. I think it took him away from his own problems for a little while. He was a good man with a big heart, and I'm sorry to say he is gone now. God bless you, George, and thank you for everything.

I had been at George's shop about a week when my old neighbor, Dave Seibert, stopped by. He had called my mother's house looking for me and was told where to find me. He told me that my children had gone to his house the night before. They had knocked on his door because they had been told to go out and play, but it was dark and they were scared. He said my son told him that he was following my instructions to go see the Seibert's if they were ever put out again. He said that he had walked them over to the house and Sandy had told him that they had gone out without her knowing and that they knew better. Dave told me that he thought Sandy was drunk and that he had thought twice about leaving the kids there, but they were already in the house. He told me that I needed to do something about it and I assured him that I would.

I called Sandy the next day and gave her a piece of my mind. I told her that I better never hear that the kids were outside alone again. She said that it was an accident and it wouldn't happen again. She promised me. I was getting to see the kids quite a bit at the time and so I didn't push it too far. But she knew that I was pissed.

The kids and I settled for what we could get, mainly weekends together, and we were having an absolute blast at Evergreen Park. We were swimming and playing and running around, sitting by the fire in the evenings roasting marshmallows and telling stories. And the kids became very good swimmers while at that park. There was a platform in the middle of the lake and we swam to it again and again. Brian was already a fairly good swimmer, but he took it to another level that summer, and Melissa would say "Daddy, wait up!" each time I got more than five feet from her, afraid that I would leave her alone. "C'mon Missy," I would say, "Swim to me!" She would kick and fling until she caught me and would put her arms around me like a vise and smile with pride. I would have to pry her off of me or swim with her locked on. She became a very good swimmer and before long she could get to the platform by herself, always with me nearby. Brian was having the time of his life, he was either swimming, riding his bike with the other kids there, or we were cooking hot dogs over a fire and telling stories.

Life had become bearable again, and just having the children made me feel whole. I was thinking less and less about their mother and becoming quite comfortable with the arrangements we had worked out. But it was also becoming more and more difficult to gather them up and bring them back to her. With their not wanting to go back home and then getting them out of the car when we got to her house, it was a real battle. Melissa would always cry, every single time. And nothing can tear your heart up more than seeing your own flesh and blood crying about something that you cannot change. Brian would play the big tough guy, never crying, just getting completely quiet and mad at the world. He would try his damnedest to be strong, but you could tell that opening the car door to get out was the last thing that he really wanted to do. Sandy would stand in the yard with a big smile on her face. I never knew if it was of happiness to see the kids again or if it was one of satisfaction from witnessing the pain.

On the last of these drop-offs, Sandy came over to the car and said that it was getting harder and harder to keep the kids happy after they had been with me. She said that they did not want to mind her and that it took several days for her to get their minds right after a visit with me. She accused me of mind-fucking them while I had them, screwing them up so that they didn't want to be with her. I told her that she had it all wrong, that I didn't put ideas in their heads while I had them. I told her that the kids just feel comfortable with me and I couldn't help that. "They know who cares and who doesn't," I said, immediately wishing I had restrained myself. Then with all the malice that she could muster, she told me that she felt it would be best if they didn't see me for a while. I yelled that I was their father and that she had better not screw with the only thing making them happy and that she damn well better not try to stop us from being together. She walked away from me screaming at the top of her lungs saying, "Don't fuck with me, Glen." As I drove away furious with her, I wondered what the ramifications were going to be.

The next day I was busy at work when George came out to my stall and asked me to come to the office. I walked into the office and was surprised to see a police officer waiting for me. He proceeded to introduce himself and said that he was with the sheriff's department. He said he was sorry to have to do this, but he was serving me papers. I was dumbfounded as he explained that my wife had filed a complaint that very morning with the Sheriffs department accusing me of sexually abusing my children. I was being served a restraining order stating that I could not be within 500 feet of my home, my children or my wife. Knocked me for a real loop, this one. Sexually abusing my children? She had gone too far now. No more nice guy.

I was furious, arguing my case with the officer who quickly interrupted me and told me how often he sees this in a divorce/ custody situation. I told him that I would never harm my kids in any way, and he advised me to just let it play out and hope for the best. "Bullshit," I told him, "It's not fair and I'm not going to hope for the best when I know this is pure bullshit,"

Now I was beyond furious. I drove to the Sheriff's department in an attempt to explain and they were sympathetic but couldn't do a damn thing to help. This was a matter for the courts, they said. They did tell me that it may probably be bullshit, but the law is designed to protect someone from possible harm and therefore proof does not have to be shown to get the order. They advised me to adhere to the restraining order and keep a clean record until the charges were either proven or dropped. Sandy had already filed for divorce and now this? I was now forced to hire my own attorney, one of the up-and-coming local lawyers referred by George, a man named

Charles Jones. I contacted him and a couple of others immediately but did not retain anyone at first because I was clinging to the hope that we would reconcile. Mr. Jones had some experience in custody cases and after telling him some of the story I chose to go with him. We cross-filed for divorce and custody and he told me to abide by the court order for the time being; since they could not prove the charges, it would only be a matter of time before the charges would have to be dropped. He knew that they could not go to court on this because it would make her divorce/ custody case look bad if they could not prove any of it and Jones trusted my word that none of it was true. While discussing the whole mess with him he said that my chances of actually winning custody of the children were about 15 percent at best. Without proving Sandy as an unfit mother or of having a drinking problem or worse, a drug problem, I had almost no hope. The fact that the kids were sent outside a few times was a beginning, but it would take more than that to prove her unfit. I told him that I wasn't willing to drag her through the mud, besides; I had my own mud puddles. I knew her as a good mother and I didn't want to make her out to be unfit, even if it was beginning to look that way.

Sandy knew when she filed the charges that she had 60 days before it would go to court and then the charges would be dropped. And she knew that for those 60 days I would not get to be with my kids, the only thing that mattered to me. Therefore it was the last and only way left that she could hurt me. She would have two months to convince them that I was a fucked up, pitiful piece of shit father that really didn't care about them or deserve them. I had a lot of time to think about that, about 60 days worth. Would they ever want to see me again after what they would be told? Would they ever believe me or trust me again? Would she tell them to say that I did things to them? Bad things?

I had a lot of time to think about an awful lot of things, the divorce, the kids, the memories that Sandy and I alone shared, all of the good and the bad times that we had gone through together. I thought about all those things and all of the memories that I could share with no one else in the world except her. Even then, with all this shit going on, I still loved her and if she would have said just once, "Forgive me and come on home," I would have gone in a heartbeat.

I could not go near her at a bar, even though I could watch or have someone else watch to see what bar she was at or when she got home. I didn't do this to keep tabs on her; I did this to try to keep tabs on the kids, trying to find out where they were each night and if they were all right, how they were being cared for and by whom. I had help, too, friends like Kay, who managed the Lawson's convenience store close to our house. Kay was someone who had come to know Sandy and myself over time, many years in fact. Over those years we had built relationships, Kay and Sandy, and Kay and I. You never think about things like that, do you? Insignificant relationships you've accumulated over time. You go to the same places a hundred times a year and you build relationships that you don't realize you have until something like this happens. Kay opened up when she realized that we were no longer together. She started by asking where Sandy was one day and I told her that we were separated, something she told me she had already figured out. She began to tell me things I would never have found out on my own, like how many times Sandy or Ralph had been coming in for beer. She started keeping track of Sandy and the kids for me. She was and still is, one of those "tell it like it is" people. She chose a side, as most friends of a couple splitting up have to do, and she chose my side.

For most of those two months Kay was my main source of information about my children. She filled me in on the news about how nine kids, including mine, were playing in the backyard of a babysitter's house and while pulling on a clothesline, they had pulled the hook loose on one end of the line and it came right out of the side of the house. It hit one of the kids in the head and the babysitter had to take the child to the hospital. It was not one of mine, thankfully, but still, it could have been, and besides, all the other children were left unsupervised while the sitter was seeking treatment for the injured one.

The kids were being moved around a lot. They were at this house one night, then another the next night, and so on. Kay told me that at one point, my kids hadn't been home, nor had they seen their mother in three days. Sandy and Ralph were having a great time. Ralph was supposedly playing in a band at a local bar, so they were out late a lot. The kids were not only being left out of my life, but Sandy's life as well. They had been relegated to pawns, to be moved on a chessboard when the time suited her needs.

CHAPTER FIVE:
A SIMPLE PLAN

Needless to say, I had the worst two months of my life. I had all that time to think about what really mattered in my life and I had to spend every one of those days without them. I lived by hearing things from other people about my own family. Can you picture anything worse?

I was still living at the campgrounds, waiting to find out exactly what pieces of my life I would wind up with. And my attorney, the prick, was doing nothing to help the situation, telling me to bide my time and eventually I would have regular visitation rights again after the bogus charges were dropped. Why wasn't he pushing for a quick hearing to show that the charges had no merit? Why wasn't he planning to get me custody of them because of the lies she had told the police? He was probably golfing with Sandy's attorney; laughing together about how they could suck all the money out of us, the bunch of blood-sucking bastards. It's funny how they file motion and then countermotion after motion and then countermotion until the money runs out and then they settle things. And speaking of sucking, my life sucked. I mean it really sucked. I was starting to wish I had been successful with the suicide attempt.

I broke down one day and called Sandy at about five in the afternoon. I figured that it would be the perfect time to reach her without pissing her off, she wouldn't still be sleeping and she wouldn't be getting ready to go out yet. I asked her how the three of them were. "We're fine Glen, you're the one you need to worry about," she said. "You need to get your head out of your ass and realize that things go the way I say they do." "I understand," I said. "I just wanted to know that the kids are all right, that's all," I told her. "The kids are fine as long as you're not around. As soon as they see you they cry and get depressed, what's that tell you?" "Well can I say hi to them?" I asked. "They aren't here," Sandy said. "Can I call back tomorrow and say hi to them?" "No, I don't want you to fuck them up by talking to them." I was getting upset now, and so I asked her how often the kids sleep in their own beds nowadays. I then interrupted the cussing by asking her why she filed charges of sexual abuse against me when she knew it wasn't true. "It was the only way that I could get you and the kids to do what you're told," she yelled. "Don't ever call here again," she said and she hung up.

My father had his own way of helping those that needed help; he would pay them to do odd jobs around his car lot. Usually they were people that had tried to buy a car from him but didn't have enough money and virtually no credit. Dad would always feel sorry for them and have them run errands or do cleanup work for him around the lot, sometimes it was paint this office or run to the junkyard to get a wheel for a car, whatever he could think of to make them feel like they were earning the money. My family often worried about that because people mistakenly thought dad was wealthy and that made us worry about someone robbing and hurting him. Half of the people you would see at his lot were people we didn't know, and some looked pretty unscrupulous. But old big-hearted Dad helped an awful lot of people that way, giving them a chance to feel like they had earned the money he was going to give them anyhow.

I spent a lot of time that summer with Dad because of my own problems and I got to know him better than I ever had. I learned a lot from him that year, more so than ever before. For a man with an eighth grade education, he was one of the smartest people I have ever known. And he also happened to have the biggest heart of anyone I ever met, even to this day. People tell me that I have a big heart, but it is small compared to my fathers.

We talked a lot as we sat there at his little car lot, he was always of the belief that justice would prevail in the end, so when we talked about my divorce and my situation with the kids he always said to just wait and see what happens. He said that in the end it would all work out for the best one way or another. I remember telling him that it was hard for me to take any comfort in that.

One day an old friend from high school came in, Willie Kindle. He was a year or two older than me and although I didn't really know him well back in school, I knew him to be a nice guy and I knew that he had married a girl from my class. He asked me how I was and we all know what we say when we're all pitiful, we tell people everything. I spilled my guts about the impending divorce, the "I can't see my kids because of her bullshit story," the "I'm miserable" and the "life sucks" part, too. I gave him the whole story in about one minute. He went white as a ghost! When he had regained his breath and could speak, he said that he was going through almost exactly the same damn thing.

Of course, we bonded in a hurry. Hell yes, misery loves company and two miserable bastards together become even more miserable, and yet, it was comforting. We went to bars and got drunk together and added that to the misery we already felt. We talked a lot though, and I came to the conclusion that Willie was an honest man, sincerely missing his family and hurting just as bad as I was. He had four children, Billy, Mandy, Bobbie and Paulie, the baby, and he said that he missed seeing them more than he did his wife. So from that point on, each time something happened to either one of us regarding our personal problems, we relayed it to the other as quickly as we could in an effort to get support or sympathy, I'm not quite sure which.

And then my lawyer called! He called me on a Friday morning. He said that there was important news and that he wanted me at his office as soon as possible. I think I was there by the time he hung up. He had just been informed that the charges were being dropped, just prior to our court date next week. I figured that both lawyers had probably decided all of this over a damn golf game; Sandy's lawyer must have lost. It was too late to set things up for this weekend, he said, but next weekend I would be allowed to see the kids. This was a shock to the senses, I had dreamed about this day, prayed for it, and yet now that it was here, I was almost disappointed. He had told me early on that since the charges were unfounded, they would have to be dropped prior to the hearing and we could possibly use this to our advantage in the divorce battle. But I had not wanted them to be dropped before the hearing; I wanted them to have to explain why they filed the charges in the first place. I wanted Sandy to be reprimanded by some judge who would understand my position and give her a major ass chewing about how shitty this whole thing was, maybe even put her in prison for the rest of her life for being a spiteful bitch from hell.

But, hey, I'll take it, I thought. I'm not a vengeful man, and all I wanted was to see the kids anyhow. I immediately went over to my mother's house to give her the good news. My parents were missing the kids as much as I was, and I knew how happy this would make them and couldn't wait to tell them. My Aunt Thelma and Uncle Cyril were over from Wales and they were disappointed that they were not going to get the chance to see the kids, and so I was very happy to give them the good news. I would be bringing the kids over the following Friday night and they would get to see them after all. They told me that they had to leave on the Saturday morning after I did get the kids and that my parents were going to be taking them back to Toronto to catch their flight home. But they would at least get to see the kids on that Friday night and have a little time with them before they had to leave. Mom was very excited and expressed her pleasure by saying that she couldn't wait, over and over, as she waltzed around from room to room, unable to stay seated. She acted like a kid on Christmas Eve. She said that we ought to ride with them to Canada that Saturday morning and then we could spend some time in Toronto together and come back when we felt like it. Mom was the first one to say that it's just a shame that you have to bring them back at all. "It's too bad that we can't drop you in Toronto and the three of you start a new life without the bitch", she said.

Actually, what mother had said was something I had already been thinking about for weeks. I should just take them when I got the opportunity and go, just move away and start a new life together. We were a family before and we could be a family again, only this time there would just be the three of us.

After telling my family the good news, I went and found Willie and told him that I would get to see Brian and Melissa in a week. And for the first time I told him that I had thoughts about taking the kids and running. Willie quickly asked me if I was serious. "Yes," I said, "I am really thinking about doing it, it would be the best thing that I could do." He said that if I did, he wanted to get his kids and go with us. And so, a simple plan began to take shape, and I decided to do just that, take them and start a new life somewhere. It wouldn't matter where. I had a trade and could make a living anywhere we happened to go.

I decided that the only way this could work was if my whole family agreed that it was the right thing to do and that they would help me and support me if I did it. I called each family member and told them that we needed to have a meeting as soon as possible at Mom and Dad's house. I told them that I was going to get the kids the following weekend and that I needed to talk to them all about something before then, and the sooner the better. All of them said that they would be at Mom and Dad's by 11 the next morning.

And so we met that Saturday morning, a meeting of the minds of all of the people that mattered to me, all of the people that I loved and that I knew loved me and my children. I told them that I was going to be allowed to have the kids the next weekend and that I was seriously considering taking them and disappearing. I had almost no chance of getting custody unless I could prove abuse or drug use in front of them, and I felt that I could give the kids a better life somewhere else than they were probably going to get if they stayed there. I told them that I was dedicating my life to being the best father that I could possibly be, whether it was as a weekend dad right there, or a full-time single father somewhere else.

I asked them each for their opinion and then listened intently. My mother was quick to say go for it; she jumped up from the table saying, "Yes, it's the best thing that you could do." My sister, Linda, also jumped up and down and started tossing out plans faster than she could write them down. And she was already making a list. "Mom, Jeanne and I will go to every yard and garage sale that we can find, buying clothes, pots and pans and anything else that we think you will need and have you ready. We'll get it done," she said. I asked the opinion of my Aunt and Uncle from Wales, and their answer was, "Do what will be best for your children. If taking them and leaving your family behind is in their best interest as opposed to leaving them here to have whatever is in store for them, then do it. Just make sure that you are doing this for them and not for yourself." Those Brits are smart, double-checking my reasoning just to make sure that I had put the kids first.

One by one my brothers agreed that it would be best for the kids if I could make this happen and give them a good home, even if it was in a different state and on the run; even if it meant not seeing each other for years to come. But we all knew that if I were to do this, I would have to do it right, because doing it and getting caught would only put the kids through more heartache and confusion. It was time to put it to a vote. And it was one vote shy of being unanimous. The only no vote was from my father, he firmly believed that the right thing to do was to stand and fight, try to win custody and live with the decision, good or bad. Dad felt that I could be mis-construed as a bad parent if I did this because it would appear to be putting my needs first before the needs of the kids. I told him that I loved him and that I respected his point of view, but that I had decided, the following weekend the children and I were going to start a new life. "We are a family," I said, "and we will be a family again." Then I told them that Willy and his kids would be going with us, and they agreed that Willy and I would be able to help each other, to make life easier for each other and that there was safety in numbers.

One of the first things Willie and I did was to buy an old brown Ford van. It was something that no one had ever seen before and just the right size to carry us and our belongings into the future, a 1968 Ford Econoline window van. Willie did some preventative maintenance on it and I hid the van in my brother Alan's barn until it was time to go. No one uttered a word about the plan as they gathered up money, clothes, pots and pans and anything else that they thought we might need. We had towels and linens, needle and thread, recipes,

Tupperware; you wouldn't believe all the things that my family gathered up for us. Everything from a first aid kit to a box full of snacks was taken care of. And they were having a blast. It was obvious to me that they were into what they were doing and they were having a great time doing it. It was a week that none of us would ever forget. I know that I will never, ever forget the effort put forth by my family, and although they were reluctant to see us go, they were concerned for our well being and gave us everything they had. They made sure that we would not do without anything for as long as possible and then some.

I spent the week working as usual and tried to not give anyone so much as a clue about what I had planned. We were all very good at it—I'm proud of them all. I knew I would need birth certificates and any school records that I could get my hands on so I went to the County office of records and asked for a copy of Melissa's birth certificate. When they said it would have to be mailed, I had no choice but to give them my parents' address. Brian was born in Massachusetts, so I called them and got the same story, they would also have to mail a copy to my parents' address once they received payment. I told mother that once they received the certificates, to wait until I called and then forward them to me wherever we were.

Then I went to see Doctor Doran to get our medical records and it was easier than I expected. I fibbed and told them that we were moving and they never questioned it because I asked for all of them, Sandy's included. I remember running into one of the local police officers on my way back to work from the doctor's office, an old friend of mine, Henry Okacik. I hadn't seen him in awhile, and he asked me what was going on with my marriage, because he had seen Sandy at several clubs while he was working security. I believe his words were, "You two aren't together are you?" I told him that it was over for us. He said that he had just gone through a nasty divorce and that he had been screwed big time, "so don't just stand there and let it happen, fight it." I smiled and told him not to worry; I wasn't going to take it sitting down. I told him that I had a plan.

On Friday, the day I was to get the kids, I worked as if it was just another normal day, collected my paycheck from the prior week, cashed it and gathered up all of my tools into a neat pile. "Just cleaning house," I told my coworkers, "just cleaning things up." I knew that I would never see any of them again, but I never let on, not even a little. It was hard to look at each one of them and know that I couldn't even say good-bye. Walking out the door and right past George Laituri and telling him to have a good weekend was even harder. Not only was he the owner, he was the closest friend I had at the shop.

Friday night at 7 p.m. exactly, I pulled into the driveway of my home. I had been sitting in my car right down the street at the convenience store that Kay ran, impatiently waiting for the agreed time to come. It was the first time in a very long time that I was allowed to go there. Sandy opened the side door and the kids came running out when they saw me. It was the best feeling a father could have. I cannot begin to explain the joy shared between us, it was obvious, too obvious for their mother. She carried two bags that included clothes, toys and some other things that she said they might need for the weekend. Sandy walked up to me and as I stood up from hugging the kids, she said, "You had better have them back here by 6 p.m. Sunday, you bastard," and pushing her finger into my chest, she said, "You better not screw their heads up either, or you'll never get to see them again." I remember giving her a simple smile and a "Yes, ma'am." I knew then that what I was about to do was the right thing; I believe that what I was about to do was God's will. As I drove away, my son said, "Thanks, Dad." I asked him why he was thanking me and he said, "For changing your mind and coming to get us." I told him that I hadn't changed my mind; nothing could stop me from getting them that day. "Mom said that you didn't ever want to see us again," he said, his voice quivering. As the tears started coming, my daughter asked me why I was crying and I told her that I was just happy to see them. We were now whole, and nothing would ever change that again. I vowed to protect them and to make this work out well and I promised God that I would be the best father in the world if he would stand beside us and help.

The evening spent at my parents' house that night was one of the toughest I have ever experienced. Most of my family was there making sure that they got to see as much of us as they possibly could, knowing that it might be the last time for awhile, possibly years. Aunt Thelma and Uncle Cyril got the chance to spend some time with the kids and we took several pictures of them together. No one but Willie and I knew where we were going; we had each sworn to tell no one. It was something we planned as well as we could, considering how little time we had and how important this was. It's harder than you think to plan something illegal; it goes against everything that you have ever learned.

Around 1 P.M. Saturday, my parents and my Aunt and Uncle left for Toronto. Mom and Dad were taking them to the airport and would see them off and then spend the night in Toronto on purpose rather than coming home. They would then leisurely drive home Sunday, arriving in the late evening only to find that we were missing. That was the best plan that we could come up with so as to keep them out of any trouble or any implication of involvement. Goodbye was ungodly hard; walking away from those who have always been there for you and always loved you was very difficult. Mother and Dad just couldn't let go of us. The crying was heartbreaking. It was a sad, sad time, but it had to happen to open the door to much happier times. My father never ever said goodbye. Ever. He used to say "It's not goodbye, it's see you later." And that's exactly what he said to me.

On Saturday afternoon I called George Laituri and told him that I needed to get some tools from inside the shop. Although I had a key, I wanted him to know that I would be there so if anyone saw me there and called him, he would know why. Besides, I didn't want to have to say goodbye to him in person; he was just too nice of a guy and with him fighting his own battle with cancer, I knew that I would probably never see him again. Two of my brothers came with me and helped me load all of my tools into a truck, and as I walked out the door for the last time, I left a goodbye note on George's desk. I knew he wouldn't get it until Monday morning and I knew he wouldn't say anything to anyone. He would be happy for me, happy for us. I thanked him for all of his help over the years and at the bottom of the note I wrote "God bless you and good luck in your battle with cancer, I pray that you will win the fight." I put his key on the note and I closed the door behind me forever.

My sister and I spent part of Saturday evening writing my goodbye letter, the letter I was to leave on my parents' dining room table for Linda to find sometime Sunday evening when she went over to feed the cats and check on things for Mom and Dad. This was of course planned by all of us; we had spent quite some time hashing out what the letter needed to say. The note told the reader that for their own good, I was taking the kids and leaving and we were starting a new life. We had a life before, but their mother decided she didn't want us to be a family, so we would be a family without her. I told them not to bother looking for us, we would no longer be using our real names and it would be fruitless to try to find us. Just know that we were a family again and that we were happy. Linda read the note Saturday evening, looked up at me and said "It's a thing of beauty. I will cry and be shocked when it is found!" We placed it on the dining room table where it couldn't be missed, exactly where everyone knew it would be. I then wrote a second letter, this one specifically to Sandy and written in the past tense, telling her what I had done and why. In it, I told her not to bother looking for us, we were starting a new life and since we were once a family and she wanted to end it, we were still a family without her. I then mailed that letter to my brother Jack down in Jacksonville, Florida, and I included a short note asking him to mail it to Sandy from down there so it would have a later date on it and a postmark from Florida. At midnight Willie drove me over to my brother Alan's house and we finished putting all of our belongings in the van. Willie was driving his 1974 cutlass and after we carried his four sleeping children from the car to the van, he stocked it full of whatever would fit. I would drive the van to my parent's house just before 1 A.M., carry my kids out and we would hit the road before anyone could see us.

Everything was a blur after that; when the time came it all happened so fast. I said goodbye to my brother Alan and his wife, Jeanne, at their house. Then I drove the two miles to my parents' house. I knew the last and hardest goodbye would be soon, Linda was waiting according to plan with my kids at Mom and Dad's. I backed into the driveway so that no one could see the license plate (I had removed the one from the front earlier), opened the side doors and ran into the house as quickly as I could. One by one I put both the children in the van alongside of Willie's sleeping kids. Then crying like the baby that I am, I hugged my sister and thanked her and told her how much I loved her and how much she meant to me. She wouldn't let go, and it seemed like we held each other in the driveway for an hour, although it was probably about a minute. And then we were gone.

We headed for the anonymity of Interstate 90 as soon as we could, the van and car filled with absolutely everything that mattered to us and we drove as fast as the speed limit would allow, wanting to put as many miles as we could between us and what was now our past. By early morning we were somewhere around Canton, Ohio, trying to get out of the state of Ohio before anything could go wrong. I remember my son waking up and asking me where we were going. I had not given a thought about what to say so I told him that we were going to see a rodeo. He was happy with that and he lay back down and patiently waited for his sister to wake up. When she did, he told her that we were far away from home and that we were going to see a rodeo. The first thing my daughter said was, "Daddy, when do we have to be back at Mommy's house?" I thought hard, and risking everything we had just done, I asked "When do you want to go back to your Mom's house?" Their answer makes me cry now while I write this, "never," they said in unison. I said okay then, you don't ever have to go back. And they were as happy as I had ever seen them. It was right then that I started my ritual of thanking God for each day with the kids. I still do. I thanked him for our first day together. Maybe it was just the first of many, or maybe it was the only one we would get.

Last photo before they left in 1981.

CHAPTER SIX:
A BREATH OF FRESH AIR

It was when we hit Kentucky that we stopped for coffee and some food. We could relax just a little bit because we were out of Ohio, where problems would likely have come from. It was the day that the kids had to be back with their mother at six. I let myself laugh one time. It was a reserved laugh.

Willie and I introduced my children to his children. We had Billy, his oldest at eight, then Brian, at seven, Melissa at six, his daughter Mandy at five, Bobby at three and the baby, Pauley at two. We had given no thought about how they would get along together, strangers bound together by our love for our children and our desire to give them a better life. We could only hope that they get to know and like each other and get along well together, we didn't have many choices.

We were going to Phoenix. We had decided to go there because no one in my family, especially Sandy, would ever expect me to go there. Willie said that he had some long lost relatives there, family that his wife didn't even know he had. They supposedly had a ranch out there somewhere and Willie was sure he could get work with them. I knew I could find work anywhere, it was just a matter of where we went and if they needed any body men. If not, the next city would do just fine. It really didn't matter to me. We didn't tell anyone anything about where we planned on going anyhow. Willie and I were the only two on the planet that knew. I figured that if anyone else knew, they could slip up, or maybe be intimidated by the police and tell them. I did not know how much of a fuss would happen after they found out we went missing, but I knew it would probably get rough.

We drove all day Sunday, getting as far away from Ohio and Pennsylvania as we could, but being very careful not to get pulled over for anything at all. Sunday night we encountered our first problem, the van was becoming harder and harder to steer. We could see that the frame had cracked on the front of the van, exactly where the steering shaft met up with it. It was too dangerous to continue without repairs, so we parked at a rest stop along the freeway and slept in both the van and the car. That night I began to realize that I was now their mother and father, it was a sobering thought and yet it felt really good. At the same time, Willie was realizing that he, too, was in the same role, and I could see the early signs of panic and fear in him.

The next morning Willie went scouting the area for a place where we could get the frame welded. He found a local home that had a sign in the front yard saying that they did welding and he came back to tell me. I carefully drove the van while Willie transported all six children and we headed to the house. A very nice lady answered the door and said that her husband was at work, but that he could certainly help us when he came home that evening. We told her that we were just passing through and had nowhere to go for the day; the truth was that we could no longer drive the van at all, so without as much as a flinch, she invited us all to stay there with her and wait for her husband to come home. She was taken aback by two men traveling with six children and everyone obviously happy. She not only fed us, she let us all shower at her house while we waited for her husband. When he came home he said that he had left his welder at a job site and that he had no way to help us that night. His wife, and I don't remember her name or I would mention it now, told him to drive back to the job site and get the welder or we would all be spending the night with them. He retrieved the welder and did the repairs that evening for us. We had to unhook the steering shaft from the front frame rail and weld the frame back together and then rehook the steering shaft. Fortunately we had all of my tools with us. When he finished I thanked him for all his efforts and gave him a hundred dollar bill. He then gave me 80 of it back, saying that we would be needing it much more than they would. As we thanked them for their help and said goodbye to our newfound friends, she handed us sandwiches and drinks for the road, including a refilled thermos of coffee. I want you to understand that these people were not well off by any means, they were just plain good people, people who were willing to go out of their way to help someone else if they believed help was needed. There are more people like that out there than you know, you just have to give them a chance and they'll open their hearts and homes and prove it to you. I don't know who they were, but I can never thank them enough for the kindness. We made it and it was because of people like them and the others that we had yet to meet.

We were a long way away by the time my parents got back Sunday night from Canada. They played their parts beautifully, as if they knew nothing about what was going on. They did it because they believed in me and what I was doing.

My sister drove over to mother's house Sunday early evening, just as planned. She would get the honor of being the one to tell Sandy the news about finding the note. The plan was for Linda to tell Sandy the news, but only after Sandy called asking about us, thereby buying us even more time. When she did, about seven o'clock, Linda told her to stop screaming at her and that she probably ought to drive over to the house, there was something there that she needed to see.

Sandy, of course, blew her lid, yelling and screaming at my parents and my sister, accusing them of being in on it and knowing exactly where we were. She left, telling them to talk me into coming back or else the shit would hit the fan and they would all be arrested for helping me plan this. None of them knew where we were going and I had told them that there would be no phone calls from me for a good while. I would assume the worst, police interrogations, wiretaps and things like that, so there would be no contact. Period.

After repairs were made to the van we continued on our way to Phoenix, stopping as needed, but trying to put more distance between home and us. We worked our way west and would stop at rest areas and let the kids run and play. They enjoyed this time together. They were getting to know each other and they were already sharing what possessions they had. We were all getting along well, I thought. Willie and I would talk whenever we had the opportunity, talk about how it was going and wondering what kind of shit was happening back home and what the future had in store for us. The future was certainly an unknown, but we were having the time of our lives right now. For the time being, we were living only for the moment. But I knew in the back of my mind that once we settled in, we would be living for whatever tomorrow held for us.

As we made our way west, the Cutlass Willie was driving decided to give out along Interstate 40 somewhere, I don't remember what state, but all we could do was leave it along the side of the road. It made things a little more difficult because now we were all in the van and there had been little room for the things Willie had stuffed into the Cutlass. We had had to make some choices right there along the side of the road, what to take and what to leave in the car because of lack of space. It was hard; everything we had packed was pretty important and very much needed. All of the kids were looking out of the back of the van and waving goodbye to the car forever as we slowly drove away and left it in the distance.

Willie was driving as we hit the Texas state line and he stopped at a small store; he said he wanted to surprise us all with something. He came out with a very large bag but wouldn't let us open it until we reached a pull off on the highway. He then stopped at a roadside spot where several picnic tables were sitting in a small group and we all got out and looked at the view. I believe he said that you could see four states from that spot. It was a beautiful scene and it was a beautiful moment and according to Willie, it called for a celebration. Willie brought out the surprise bag and we celebrated with Twinkies, a yellow meat watermelon and cans of pop for all the kids. Willy and I toasted the moment with a can of Coors, my first can ever. Just one can each. It was the first time that I had ever even heard of Coors. We toasted our newfound freedom along the side of the road at a picnic table and that night I thanked God for another day.

We kept going, each city or town a new experience for us and before we knew it we were in Phoenix. It was so hot that we had to take the windows out of the sides of the van just to get some airflow, and even then it was stifling hot. The van didn't have air-conditioning; heck, most cars from up north didn't. So there we were in Phoenix, driving around town trying to find a contact, a starting point, a new beginning, and sweating like a bunch of pigs. With the relentless heat came the first arguing and complaining from the kids, it was an impossible situation, being in Phoenix in August, in a van with eight people, with no air-conditioning and no home.

We pulled in to a K.O.A. campground and settled in for the night; two guys, six children and one van with all the side and rear windows removed. We parked in one of those spots where an RV parks and opened all of the doors on the van. We had two picnic tables, a small barbecue grille and the van, what else could you possibly need? The campground had a pond, a swimming pool, showers and a store. I looked at the phone in the office and resisted calling my parents. I wanted so badly to tell them that we were safe and that we were where we had planned to go, but I couldn't risk it. I wanted to put there minds at rest and I just couldn't.

Man, we had it all. I remember asking my two kids that first night if there was anything that they needed and with hugs from each of them, they said no. Willie slept on one picnic table and I slept on the other. We lined them up behind the van so that no one could get in or out of the van without crawling over one or both of us. It was hot, it was uncomfortable and it was crowded, but the kids were clean and fed. They had run around and played and we had gone swimming. I had read them all a story and they were content. There was very little complaining from them considering we had uprooted them from life as they knew it and tossed them all together in a pile in a strange place and in ungodly heat. They were living what was to them a vacation and they loved it. And as I fell asleep that night lying on a picnic table, I thanked God for another day with my children.

The next morning, Willie and his children took off in search of his long lost family. He knew that he had some relatives there; he just had to track them down. Brian, Melissa and I stayed at the park. Everything we owned was in the boxes stacked on or next to our picnic tables because Willie was driving around in our home, and my tool box, my only way to earn a living, was covered by a sheet next to a picnic table. We swam and played all day until they came back with the good news, he had found an Aunt and Uncle and they had offered to put Willie and his kids up for the time being. They had also told Willie that they had a small camper on the back of their pickup truck and that my kids and I were welcome to drive the truck and live in the camper at the park for the time being. It was great news! We felt that things were falling into place and I felt that God was without a doubt on our side. The fact that we hadn't been caught yet was already proof enough for me.

When we first met Willie's aunt and uncle, Gary and Paulette (Pep) Dempsey and their daughter, they could see that every one of us had a rash pretty much all over our body. We realized that as soon as we had removed all of the windows from the van, the air rushing in had started blowing fiberglass insulation all over and it stuck to our sweaty bodies, giving us all a rash. I'll bet we looked like hell. It was nice of them to take care of us and feed us and offer their camper to us, two men and six kids showing up at their door out of nowhere needing all the help that they could get.

Willie and his four kids moved in with Gary and Pep and their daughter, and the three of them were immediately sworn to secrecy. The last thing we needed was for someone to catch wind of where we were. The kids and I stayed at the campground and used the camper truck offered to us. It made things much more comfortable for us. It had a small refrigerator and that helped us out a lot, we could keep milk and have cereal for breakfast. I slept on a picnic table that I pushed up against the back door of the camper each night, and the kids slept in the camper with the back door and the two small side windows open for air flow. It was a very small camper and even with the door and windows open it was still hot, but we made do with what we had. Not one of us complained. In fact it was our only option. The only real glitch was the night Melissa rolled over in her sleep and fell out of the sleeper bunk and caught her chin on the edge of the table in the camper as she fell. The thud woke me up quickly and the screaming woke several other campers up nearby. With the first aid kit supplied by my family and the help of a couple of fellow campers, we got her taken care of. She was a trooper though and she still bears the scar under her chin because I couldn't afford to pay for the stitches that she really should have gotten. Besides, taking her to an emergency room would probably expose us right off the bat and we didn't need that.

The following day was a Friday, and I drove the truck around Phoenix looking for work. I was told to drive down a street named Camelback and that's where I would find car dealerships. I stopped at five places that day, each time walking in with both of my kids and applying for a body man position. I had no idea if anyone needed a body man or not, it would depend on how busy the shops were and if they had enough help. All I could do was apply and hope one of them would give me a chance, just let me begin to earn a living again. We drove back to the campgrounds that evening and I left word in the office that I had been giving the campground phone number out as the only way to reach me. We swam most of the evening and almost all of the weekend as well. We weren't used to that kind of heat, and so the best place for us was in the water. Willie and the kids spent most of the time with us at the campgrounds, and we grilled hot dogs and played a lot. The kids took it all just like we were camping out and they had a good time with it.

The following Monday we took off again in search of more dealerships so that I could find work as soon as possible. What money we had was starting to run low and I would be forced to take any type of job soon if no one was hiring body or paint help. The kids and I found a note stuck to our picnic table when we got home that evening. It asked me to come to the office when I could. The lady working in the office was beginning to know us and was aware that I desperately needed to find a job. With a big smile she handed me a small pile of names and numbers. I had been offered a job at four dealer-ships all in one day. "We need to celebrate," she said. I stayed calm and reserved as I thanked her for being the bearer of good news and then after the kids and I walked out of the door, I broke out in the biggest grin ever, looked straight up, and said, "Thank you, Lord." The next morning the three of us drove to each one of the dealerships just to see how far they were from the camp. Something about Courtesy Chevrolet on Camelback seemed to feel right, I couldn't really tell you why, and I chose it even though it was one of the farthest away.

Howard Florence was the manager and I got a good feel-ing about him right from the start. I told him that I had a few custody issues that were being worked out and I asked him to keep me aware of any strange phone calls or inquiries about me should the office get any. In return, I promised that I would work hard and never disappoint him or make him regret hir-ing me. I had worked there just a day or two when another employee came up and introduced himself. His name was John Moore. He said that he had heard that I was a single parent and that we were living at a campground. After I told him we had just moved here from up north and needed to make a new start, he said, "Follow me." We walked to the front of the deal-ership and up a flight of stairs to what must have been the accounting department and he asked to see a particular woman. He spoke to her quietly for a couple of minutes and then I heard him tell the lady to write me a check for $475 and he said that if I didn't stay there long enough for them to pay-roll deduct it back from me that he would pay it back himself. As we walked out of the office together, me holding the check in my hand, he said "now go find a place to live." I was stunned. I could not find the words to thank him, nor could I speak without beginning to cry. He patted me on the shoulder and said "Don't say anything, just try to stay here long enough to pay them back." How do you say thank you all these years later? John told me that there was another man that worked there that was having similar problems, but that he was on vacation. "Just wait until you meet Jerry," he said.

I wound up renting a house on North 38th Place in Paradise Valley; I remember it as if it were yesterday. The electric was already on and was included in the rent, so that was the reason why I chose the house. The problem was with getting the gas turned on. I did not want my name on anything that could be easily tracked and so we moved in with no gas. The oven was gas as was the water heater, so cooking was a problem, but not as much of a problem as showering was. We had to take turns showering in cold water and if you have never done it, it's a real experience. It takes some getting used to. Brian learned to be okay with it; he would just make it quick and come out shivering. But Melissa, she would raise hell about it every time. I would always have to shower first to show them that it wasn't so bad, and then Brian would go and finally, after putting it off as long as she could, Melissa would take her turn. It would tear my heart out each and every time, I felt so bad for them because I knew how cold it felt. But it had to be and what has to be will be. The cooking thing was pretty easy to remedy, we just grilled out in the backyard every night. The only problem with that were the spiders; there were lots of spiders all over the place. I think that they were black widows but I'm not sure. They had little fiddles on their stomachs and would lunge at us when we tried to kill them.

We had no refrigerator, no furniture, no beds and of course, no television. We did have a stove, but we couldn't use it. And believe it or not, we were happy. We loved it; it was us, just us, and it was very good. We slept together on the floor in one of the bedrooms. I had made a large square in the middle of the room by lying fully opened sleeping bags down and covering that with some blankets. Most of what we ate was cooked on the grille, other than cereal and sandwiches. I took the cover off of an air-conditioning vent in one of the rooms and I would keep some perishable things inside the opening in an attempt to refrigerate them. I kept it cold in the house for three reasons, we didn't have to pay for the electric, the cold air was our refrigerator and it was just horribly hot there. Pep and Gary's daughter started coming over in the evening once in a while and would help me do things. She would take what little laundry that we had and clean it for us and she would help with small things just to make our lives a little better and I thank her for it now because I probably didn't get the chance as we were leaving. Heck, I can't even remember her name.

Willie and his kids showed up at our house one day and asked if they could move in with us, and I said, "Yes, of course." They were already wearing out their welcome with Gary and Pep, and Willie mentioned that they were beginning to ask about their truck. Willie was a good man but was overwhelmed by having twice as many kids as I had and less natural ability to deal with them than I had. I'm not knocking him in any way, he just had more problems than I and his were more difficult to deal with. The baby was a handful all by himself and then with the other three kids and the fact that his reason for leaving with me turned out to be quite a bit different than my own, he truly had more than he had bargained for. He was overwhelmed and almost ready to tilt. It turned out that Willie's reason for leaving was completely different than mine. He took his four children and left simply to get his wife back; I left with my two children to start a new life without my wife. As time went on, the differing viewpoints, and the decisions that those viewpoints led to, became obvious and it split us apart.

Willie and the kids moved in with us as a matter of convenience for us all. I already had a job, but finding someone to watch the kids each day so that I could work was already a problem. I was dropping them off in the mornings at the camp-ground because the lady that we knew that worked there had volunteered to watch them until I could come up with a better plan. We returned the truck to Gary and Pep Dempsey and I thanked them for its use and for all of their help. I felt com-pelled to apologize for our barging into their lives as we did.

Willie still had no job, although his promise of getting a job quickly was the reason we had decided on Phoenix in the first place. Moving them in meant life would be easier for them and easier for me as well. But it wasn't easier for Brian or Melissa and it didn't last very long; again the differences between us were obvious. Willie was buying time, always talk-ing about or thinking about his wife, trying to teach her a lesson, and I was building a new life for us, a life with no plans to go backward and no thoughts of my wife except the fear of being caught. I sometimes wondered what Sandy was feeling, but it was not something that I took any pleasure in. Willie was calling his wife almost daily; something that I knew would get us in big trouble sooner or later. I was calling no one; not one person from our past knew where we were.

Our little arrangement began to fall apart quickly. Willie would either let me take the van to work and leave them with-out any transportation at all, or everyone would have to ride in the van while Willie dropped me off at work. It was very diffi-cult for me to say goodbye to my children and watch them drive away in the van knowing that they were out of my con-trol and exposed to whatever the others dealt them. Each time this happened I wondered if they would be caught while I was at work and seeing them drive away would be the last time I ever saw them. It was hard to focus at work, my thoughts always with my children.

I would get home from work and although combined we

had very little, what we did have would be strewn all over the house. Walking in and finding dirty diapers on the kitchen counter and all the food gone was bad enough, but being told the kids had been fighting and mine were the problem was pretty much the end of it.

I came home one day and Willie told me that my son had marked our territory by telling his son that it was our house, not theirs, and that they couldn't keep doing what they were doing to the place anymore. Willie asked me what I was going to do about it. I told him that I agreed with my son and that they had to change the way they live or they would need to get out. Willie grabbed his kids and said that they had to leave, but the only vehicle that we had was the van, so I told him to take it and they gathered up their stuff and they left.

I don't mean to imply that Willie and his kids were bad, they were not, what happened was the culmination of the differences between us; it was as simple as that. Willie was a good man with a big heart and I respect him even now for what he took upon himself in an effort to get back the woman that he loved, and although I did not know it until many years later, he did get her back and they became a family again.

Willie had taken the van and we had no means of transportation. But I had the house. Ironic, isn't it? We had a place to live but no wheels, and they had a way to move around but no home. We were here to stay, I thought, and he was on the move, wanting so desperately to go home to his wife. Willie had called her many times, always hoping she would say "come home," and surely that would draw attention to us all pretty soon. I had called no one and did not intend to for any reason. Any calls to home would have only caused stress for my family because by now the police were certainly looking for us and I did not want anyone in my family questioned to the point of giving in and divulging our whereabouts. I was thinking about possible wiretaps on phone lines and I wanted to be sure that our new life was as secure as it could be. The only thing that was of any comfort to me at the time was my knowing that Sandy didn't know who Willie was. Since she was in Ohio and Willie's wife, Jean, was in Pennsylvania, they had no reason to put us together. The only people that knew we were together were my family, and I knew that they wouldn't tell a soul.

It was a lonely time. After catching a ride home from work we were pretty much stuck there with no car. It was way too hot to walk very far and we only walked to a store if it was an emergency. After the kids were put to bed and all the stories were read, it was a somber life I had, plenty of time alone to reflect and judge myself and my actions. Plenty of time to ponder the future and to wonder if I was making a big mistake, yet always trying to plan and be prepared for whatever may happen next. Have all of our bases been covered? Have I made any mistakes that could cost me my children? Have I done the right thing for them?

Chapter Seven:
The Flip of a Nickel

I was extremely lucky I guess, everything always seemed to go my way. I didn't know if it was because I had God on my side and I was doing what was right, or if I was just one lucky bastard. But things just always worked out for us rather than fall apart. When Willie and the kids left, I had no one to watch the kids and then out of nowhere, a friend of Pep's offered to watch them. Her name was Sherry Weaver. Her husband's name was Gary and they were friends of Gary and Pep's that we had met at Pep's one day. They lived pretty close to where we did in Paradise Valley. I had to trust her, I simply had no other choice except to go back to the lady at the campground and impose on her again. Besides, the lady at the campgrounds had made a pass at me and the last thing I needed at that time was a woman in my life. I was bitter toward women in general already because at the time they seemed nosey and either just had to know where my wife was, or they looked at me as if I was incapable of raising my children properly. But Sherry was wonderful with my children and for some reason she trusted and believed in me. John Moore from work was picking me up in the mornings and bringing me home until I could get enough money together to buy a car. It was all working out.

Howard Florence told me that he had a 1974 Chevy Impala that he would sell me for $800. But that was a lot of money at the time and I was paying back the money I had been advanced at work. I had no choice but to break down and call my father and ask if he would wire me the money. Being without transportation was making life hard on us, but more importantly, in our position it was giving me no means of escape should I need to. When I spoke to my father that day he was extremely happy to know that we were okay and he told me that Sandy had moved out of our house and in with Ralph the day after we left. He also told me that she had had the phone disconnected at our house that same Monday. It seemed to me that not only did she not want to hear from me; she wanted to make sure she didn't hear from me. And later she had shown up at my brother Jack's house in Florida along with the police looking for us. She had received my goodbye letter mailed from Florida and assumed that we could be found there. I guess there had been quite a scene out there, my brother being a hard-core, not-afraid-of-anything kind of person. He told them all to get the hell off his property unless they had a search warrant. Years later he would be saying the very same thing to the police at my parents' house.

In early September, Sandy and her friends were trying desperately to find any shred that could lead them to our whereabouts and my mother had reason to believe that someone had been in her home while they were out one day. She was positive that someone had rummaged through the trash; it had been picked apart while out by the street. So together with my sister, Linda, and my favorite sister-in-law, Jeanne, they set out to place as many worthless clues as possible everywhere. They even used this one on a letter that they pretended to send out; Monsieur Saccade, Noranda, Quebec, Canada. I wonder if they ever figured out that the French word *Saccade* means jerk. The letter was to a Mr. Jerk in Canada.

I had Dad send the money to a nearby Western Union, and I was very nervous about picking it up, assuming that the law could be there watching for me. If they were listening to the phone call they would know where to find me. But I had no choice; I had to do it. And after watching the building for a long, long time, I realized that no one was there looking for me and I collected the money and left.

With the money I bought the car and we now had a means to get around and with a house, a car and an income, things were working out well. I was soon finished paying back the money to the dealership and Sherry was just great with Brian and Melissa. She was watching them each day for me and she began to love them like the mother they didn't have.

But it was now time for school to start and the next hurdle was enrolling the kids somehow. I went to the local grade school, Indian Bend Elementary, and told them that we had just moved to Phoenix and the move was so sudden that I had had no time to get their school records but had sent for them and they should be here soon. I never told them anything about custody problems because I did not want to cause anymore suspicion than I needed to. Brian was entering third grade and Melissa first, so there was no big deal about the records, how big could these records be anyway? With medical records and birth certificates in hand, all they needed was a few shots and they were in. And in just a few days, the teachers at Indian Bend had made my children feel like they belonged there. I want to thank them for the compassion shown to Brian and Melissa regarding our sudden move, the extreme heat that we were not accustomed to, and the tears shed while walking into a new school and away from their daddy, their only form of comfort at the time.

I began to drop the kids off at Sherry's house in the morning and I would head for work and Sherry would walk the kids to school and then pick them up. It couldn't have worked out any better. I was making as much money as I could and we were slowly building a support system around us, a system that should we need it, hopefully would help us hide or disappear again if we should ever need to. And although I didn't know it, we would need to soon.

The guys I worked with were the greatest bunch of people I could have asked for. I had John, the man who had guaranteed my advance money and another body man there named John Lewis, this one being much younger than the other John. They had a bond between them that I could feel and yet they acted like they hardly knew each other. I was curious about them but never asked questions, I had my own problems to worry about. They would both assume positions of responsibility over me and look out for me; even to the point of setting up an escape route for me should it ever be needed. There was also Jerry Smith, the one that was on vacation when I first started, and after he met me he too, became an ally. When Jerry came back from vacation, John Lewis had brought him straight to me and he had introduced us. The first thing that Jerry did was pull out his wallet and peel off about $300 and hand it to me. He said that he had already been told that I had paid back the money from the dealership and he said that he was sure that I could use it to help the kids. He insisted. Jerry took to me instantly and I later learned that it was because he respected what I was doing, something he had considered doing himself, but as of yet, hadn't. He was in the middle of a custody battle of his own.

God only knows why all these people helped me. I was there just long enough to tell them my story and muck up their lives with my problems. I had to apply for an Arizona driver's license shortly after I had started at the dealership, and my fears that that information would be relayed to Ohio were about to come true. I put it off as long as I could, knowing that after I had done so, that it would be just a matter of time before someone found out where we were, my gut told me so. I told my trusted new friends about my fears and they agreed that it could probably happen and so they set up escape plans and routes for us. I told them that it's always better to be prepared.

And it didn't take long. All told, I had been in the city of Phoenix a total of about seven weeks when it happened. I was working in my stall about three quarters of the way back in the body shop when John Lewis came around the corner and said that the police were in the office asking if I was there. The office people would have to say yes, but were stalling just long enough for word to get to me so that I could follow the planned escape route over the fence at the back of the body shop. My heart dropped and it took just a second for stunned silence to turn to total fear and in an instant I was running as fast as I could. No one went with me, no one helped me over the fence, it was planned that if it should happen, no one would jeopardize themselves, but instead stay where they were and stall for time if possible. I went over the fence in a swan dive and was on my way to my children. I'm not sure if I even used the ladder that they had placed there for me.

I drove straight to Indian Bend Elementary and told the people in the office that there was an emergency in the family and that we needed to go back home to Ohio. Once I had the kids, I dropped them at Sherry's house and quickly went to our house to gather up as much of our things as I could. But paranoia got the best of me and I left behind almost everything that we had. If they knew where I worked, it wouldn't take but a matter of minutes to find out where we lived and get there. After I picked the kids up from Sherry's house, we did what we always did when I needed to think. We would always go to a place where we could blend in and I could think and yet the kids could play, a McDonalds. I waited for Jerry to get home from work and I called him as planned. The police had walked the property and had left scratching their heads. But now they knew that we were there and the dealership had had no choice but to give them my correct address and that meant that they were already at the house and probably staking it out. All of this also meant that Sandy probably now knew where we were. If not, she soon would.

I headed for Jerry's house as planned; he lived very close to Sun Devil Stadium in Tempe, just outside of town. He had a good-size house and a small apartment above the garage that was empty at the time and we had arranged for it to be a safe house for us if it were ever needed. As I drove over to Jerry's place I watched every police car that I saw, ready to head straight out of the city if need be and leave all of my tools, my only way to make a living, behind. But there was no notice of us. Jerry said the police had not asked what I was driving and no one at the dealership had offered to tell them. But I knew that it wouldn't take them long to find that out either, and we needed to park the car and hide.

We stayed at Jerry's garage apartment for about 10 days, I guess. It was hard to tell time because I was in a fog through this whole thing. It was really hell on earth. I never knew if the police would show up at Jerry's place or not. All it would take was one person to say something to someone and it would be over, or one cop to stop me as I drove to wherever I was going. During that time, little by little, Jerry had brought all my tools to the house. The other guys at work had helped him load them up and get them to me. I had gone on a couple of trips to find an attorney to talk to and I finally found one that was very helpful. He told me about a *Nationwide Uniform Custody Agreement,* and that there were six states that did not honor or abide by that agreement. He even gave me the names of the six states, well sort of; he wrote them down on a piece of paper and excused himself to get us coffee. He said that he could not condone what I was doing, but going to one of those six states would probably be to my advantage should I eventually get caught. Common sense told me that the best way to get lost would be to go to the biggest state of the six and disappear again and it was easy to figure out which state that was. For the total price of 10 dollars, I now knew where we had to go, and we had to get there as fast as we could.

On October 2nd, 1981, Brian's eighth birthday, I set my sights on Texas, a state I had never envisioned myself ever going to. Of course I couldn't tell anyone, not even the kids. I had bought Brian a racecar set for his birthday, one with about five feet of oval looping track and a couple of cars. I gave it to him that afternoon along with a small cake and that is how we celebrated his birthday. Jerry and his two boys came over and had birthday cake with us that evening. When finished, we had to say goodbye to them and I thanked Jerry from the bottom of my heart for the help and hospitality that was shown us during our brief stay in Phoenix. After they left, we sat on the floor of the apartment and played with Brian's new toy for quite a while, the three of us, and under the circumstances, we were happy. It was happiness in its simplest form, three people who loved and trusted each other, about to head into the unknown again together.

Later that night I told the kids that we should get some sleep and in the morning we would head out to our new home. They asked where we were going and I couldn't tell them yet, but I promised I would tell them as soon as we pulled out. I just couldn't risk them saying anything to anyone in case Jerry or one of his kids came back over. The kids were all wound up and saying that they were not sleepy and they asked me if we could leave right away instead of in the morning. They promised me that they would keep me awake all night if we left now. I think that they just wanted to know where we were going, but it made sense, leave now while it was dark and take advantage of the night. And so we did. We pulled out of Jerry's driveway and I told the kids that we were moving to Texas. That made them happy, so happy that by the time we got onto Interstate 10 and headed east they both fell asleep. I drove all night with them asleep next to me on the front seat. And as I drove and sipped my cup of coffee, I looked at the two of them and said, "Thank you, Lord, for another day." It had been a little more than eight weeks.

I look back now and think about how we must have looked to other travelers along the way; we had the backseats of the car tied to the roof, tool boxes hanging out of the open trunk, and the trunk lid tied down as best I could. We had all of my tools piled where the backseat bottom would have been and all of our belongings were in boxes on top of the tools. The only room we had was the front seat and with two sleeping children, it was a little tight. I drove all night, heading east as fast as I could without risking being pulled over. Once we were out of Arizona and in New Mexico, I could take my first relaxed breath. We stopped and ate when we needed to, parked in rest areas and slept when we needed to and we kept on going. We had a good time on that trip. We counted how many different state license plates that we could find, we sang songs and took turns whistling, whatever we could do to occupy time. Of all the good things that I can remember about our entire adventure, that trip was one of the most special memories that I have and cannot share with anyone, the kids were too young and don't remember it and there was no one else to share it with but God.

By the time we crossed into Texas I was exhausted. Between the driving and the fear that comes with being wanted, always watching every police car that you see, I had worn myself out. We made it to a small town just east of El Paso called Van Horn and we checked into a motel for the night. I can remember the sense of relief I felt knowing that we had made it to Texas and the anonymity it would hopefully provide us. And then a critical thing took place in that small motel room that night, one of those things that will affect the rest of your life. After we showered, ate and slept, I took out a nickel and flipped it so that it would land on the bed, heads would mean Dallas and tails would mean Houston. It was tails. We were moving to Houston, and no one on the face of the earth knew it except the three of us. The kids were so happy. It didn't matter to them where we went, as long as we went together. And according to Brian, going to Houston was perfect; we could really go see a rodeo like I told them when we first left Ohio.

CHAPTER EIGHT:
HELLO HOUSTON

It takes a lot of driving to get from Van Horn, Texas, to Houston and I must have looked over at those two sleeping angels next to me on the seat over a hundred times. I hoped and prayed that what I was doing was right.

It was about 8 a.m. when we got there, and as we came into town I noticed how awful the traffic looked. I had never seen so many cars going so slow on such a big freeway. I exited at Highway 6 and immediately pulled into a Jack in the Box, nervous about all the traffic and more than ready for a cup of coffee. As I paid for the coffee at the drive-in window, I asked the girl if something had happened up on the freeway. She asked me why I was asking, and I pointed to all of the cars everywhere. She smiled and said that it's like that every day here, there's nothing wrong. I told her that we had just pulled into town and that we planned on living here and I asked her if she knew where I could go to find some car dealerships. She advised me to keep driving east on the freeway and I would find plenty of them. I also asked her what parts of town had the best schools and without any hesitation, she said that Aldine and Alief had the best schools in the area. I thanked her for the help and pulled into a parking spot.

I sat in the car and sipped my coffee while I waited for the traffic to clear up. She had said that it would die down after about 8:30, so I took the time to relax. At about 9 a.m. I woke the kids up and brought them into the restroom of the restaurant and we all cleaned up as best as we could before we headed toward our future. Even after the traffic had let up, it was still bad enough to make anyone nervous and as tired as I was it was pretty damn scary. I wasn't used to so many cars coming from every direction and everyone in a hurry and apparently mad about something. I kept driving east, passing about 10 car dealerships until I saw a Chevrolet dealership on the right-hand side of the freeway that for some reason seemed to be calling my name. The place was Courtesy Chevrolet, and as I pulled in I knew that this was the right place. I just felt it in my heart. Maybe it was because it had the same name as where I had worked in Phoenix, although I knew it was just coincidental. I don't know how I knew that it was the right place, but I knew it.

I pulled in and asked for the body shop and was directed to the rear of the dealership where I parked the car and walked in with both kids alongside me, hand in hand. We walked into the office and I asked for the manager. A tall man just a couple of years older than me walked up to us and introduced himself as the manager. I liked him the moment I shook his hand, the handshake strong and direct. His name was Phil Crosby and he had a smile on his face that came with genuine sincerity. He had a distinct Southern drawl, and I assumed that he was a local because I had never heard that accent before. I told him that I had just pulled into town and was looking for a job as a body man and painter. I introduced the two kids to him and told him that it was just the three of us and that all my tools were in my car and if he would give me a small job to do, I would show him my ability and if he was satisfied, he could hire me and if not, I would go somewhere else. Mr. Crosby looked at me and smiled broadly and said, "Well now, you're pretty doggone sure of yourself, aren't you?" I remember smiling back and answering with a "Yes sir, I am." He shook his head, grinned from ear to ear, put his hands on his hips and said, "Okay, you've got the job. I can't turn down somebody with your kind of attitude."

I told him that we literally had just hit town and that we had to go find a place to live and that I needed to enroll the kids in a school as soon as possible. I told him it could take me a couple of weeks before I could actually start and if he couldn't hold the job for me that I would understand. He smiled that broad smile of his again and said "Son, you sure drive a hard bargain, but don't worry about it, you've got enough to worry about right now. Just handle what you need to handle and you'll have a job when you get here. What do you want to do here—do you want to fix cars or paint them?" he asked. I told him that where I came from we fix them and paint them, and he said, "It's not that way down here. You can fix them or paint them but not both." I told him that I would rather fix them because I could make money more quickly by fixing cars than I could by painting them. I was very picky about my paint work and it tended to slow me down and right now I need to make as much money as I could get my hands on.

There was one last favor that I had to ask him for; I really needed to unload my tools and toolboxes to free up space in the car. He shook his head again before he agreed to that and then he got a couple of people to help me unload. We got out the toolboxes that were hanging out of my trunk and I threw all of my tools into the drawers and pushed the tools up alongside a wall of the shop. And then I put the seats back where they belonged. With a few handshakes and a couple of thank you's, we were gone.

On the way to Courtesy Chevrolet we had passed a motel that had advertised rooms for about $24.99 a night. It was the cheapest I had seen and I knew how to find it so I headed back west and we checked in. I asked the woman at the motel if we were anywhere close to the Aldine or Alief areas and she said that Alief wasn't too far away, just south of there she said. And then the kids and I checked into our room, unloaded some boxes of things and took showers. They were our first showers since Van Horn and boy did it feel good. It was an exciting time for us, we were now in Houston, Texas, and we had a lot to look forward to already. I reminded myself that we also had a lot of reasons to look behind us. Either I was the luckiest man alive, or God was with us every move we made and I was positive that what I was doing was pleasing Him.

Within two hours of hitting town, I had a job and we had a general area to focus on to find a good place to live with good schools. We couldn't help but celebrate. Our first night in Houston we did what we always did—we found a McDonalds with a playground and we ate and they played under my never wavering eye until they were exhausted. That night we got back to our room and the three of us passed out.

The next day we began learning our way around the city a little. I drove until I found Alief, a small suburb of Houston in the southwest corner. It seemed to be a nice area. It was clean, the people that we noticed seemed nice and the schools we passed looked to be almost new. I had very little money and I knew that it would not last long, so I immediately began stopping at apartment complexes and asking about monthly rent and down payment costs. All of them wanted more for a deposit than I was willing to part with; the money that I had needed to last until my first paycheck and that wasn't going to happen until we had a place to live. After two nights at that motel I had to move us to another motel closer to the Alief area and cheaper to stay at. I knew that the money was slowly going to run out and that I had to conserve what we had left as best as I could. The Motel 6 near the intersection of highway 59 and Bissonnet offered a weekly rate a little cheaper than the first place and would save us some money, so there we went. I was paying by the week and knew that we had little time before we would be broke. We had a swimming pool and it was terribly hot and humid, so if we weren't out looking for somewhere to live, we were swimming, just like we did in Phoenix. The humidity was the worst that we had ever known.

We began to make a few friends almost immediately. There was the Haynes family further down in the motel; we met them at the swimming pool and then my kids wanted to play with their kids afterwards. They had just moved to Houston from Illinois and were in the very same boat that we were in, except that they had several more children than I had. Shortly after meeting Chuck and Lori and their kids, they invited us to have supper with them one evening in their motel room. I remember them asking me a lot of questions about why I was a father with two kids but there was no mother, and I told them that the mother was very confused right now and had wanted to go her own way for awhile and experience other things. I wanted to just tell them that my wife had passed away; it would have been easier, but I opted not to say such a horrible thing. "We were new at being a three member family but we would be just fine, I already had a job, we just needed a place to live and a school and we would be set," I said. They were in worse shape than we were with four kids to feed. They had no home, no job offers and they were also about out of money. And yet there they were, feeding us, and it was home cooked food, too. I told them that the next night supper would be on us at our room.

There was also a guy that was about my age who stood outside of his motel room a lot, just smoking and watching. He seldom wore a shirt and it seemed to me that he didn't have a job either. I cannot remember his name, but he actually turned out to be a pretty nice guy. One day he said hello and asked me about how we wound up at that motel and we began to get to know each other. I found out that they were in the same situation as the rest of us; they had moved from Alabama with his girlfriend and her two redheaded daughters. He too, needed to find a job and a place to live. It turned out that his girlfriend was a dancer in a topless club, so they at least had an income because she was already working and bringing home cash every night while he watched the kids and got them to sleep. That explained why he was always looking out toward the pool— their two redheaded girls were swimming and he was watching them from the upstairs balcony.

And there were others. We were all in the same boat, all of us new to Houston and looking to start a new life, hopefully a better life than the one we were leaving behind us. All of us wound up at the same cheap motel at the same time and in the same condition, with no family, no friends, no jobs and almost broke. It was a huge melting pot of new Houstonians scraping and clawing for a new life.

As usual, I got the first break. An apartment complex on Boone Road, called Brays Village Apartments, had agreed to let me into an apartment with $150 down and the promise of a job. The lady actually called Phil Crosby to confirm that I really did have a job waiting for me. She said that they were not allowed to let anyone move in unless the first month's rent was paid in full, but because of our circumstances she would. I think that the only reason I got it at all was because of the three of us sitting there in front of her looking so desperate and so pitiful. I didn't quite know why she had bent the rules for us, but I was glad to get it and it was perfect for us. It was in Alief and right next to Chancellor Elementary school and only about five miles from the motel. What else could I possibly want? They would have to put us in a one-bedroom apartment for a couple of weeks until a two-bedroom became available, but so what, we didn't have enough belongings to fill a closet let alone an apartment, so a one-bedroom would be just fine. It was about October 12th; we had been in Houston for something like eight days and we had a place to live, a good school in a good district, and I had a good job waiting for me. It was starting to work out perfectly for the three of us.

We went back to the motel that afternoon and told all of our new friends about our good fortune. They asked where the place was and if I thought that they had any chance of getting in there and all I could say was go ask them and find out, ask for Diana, she's the one who cut us a break and helped us.

The next day Chuck came back to the motel and walked right up to me and said thanks. Not only did they get a three-bedroom apartment at Brays Village, but he had been hired as a maintenance man there. They would be moving in before us because they needed him so badly. And the guy who stood around the motel while his girlfriend danced at clubs also went there. He came back to the motel saying that they were going to get the one-bedroom apartment that we were about to move into as soon as we moved out of it and into our two-bedroom apartment in a few weeks. It was perfect; everything was working out better for all of us than we could have planned. It was as if the kids and I were being taken care of by a higher power and everyone around us was going to be helped as well. And every night I thanked God for another day and counted the number of days that we had now been together.

And so the children and I moved into the one-bedroom apartment soon after and I immediately signed them into Chancellor Elementary school, a wonderful school less than two blocks from the apartments. I told the people at the school that we had just moved to Houston from Phoenix and that their school records from Indian Bend Elementary would be forthcoming. I didn't tell them that those records would be virtually

blank, we had not been there long enough for the kids to estab-
lish any records and the ones from Ohio, which Indian Bend
Elementary in Phoenix was still waiting for, would never come.
The people at the school were great about it though and they
had no reason to believe anything was less than legitimate. I told
them that the children's mother and I were in the middle of a
custody dispute and although she had deserted us, she could surface one day and try to steal the kids from me. It was a white lie,
but in a way she had deserted us by forsaking us. They asked me
if I had started the process to get legal custody of the children
and I told them that yes I had, in Phoenix, but I had been
warned that she was coming to find us and steal the children and
that explained why we were now in Houston. I told them that I
had already spoken with an attorney in Houston and that we
would be filing for permanent custody in Harris County, Texas,
as soon as we had established residency, another tiny white lie.

They marked the files of Brian and Melissa with asterisks
and asked me to fill out papers designating who could have the
legal right to pick up or remove them from school and at the
time there was no one but me. I told them that as soon as I had
made other arrangements I would come by and provide that
information.

We were in our own place, finally. The two kids slept in
sleeping bags on the floor in the bedroom and I slept on a
sleeping bag in the spot where a couch would have been if you
had one. The kids each had one suitcase next to their sleeping
bag and in it was an assortment of things that they felt comfortable with. In Brian's case it was comic books and his
favorite toys and in Melissa's case, it was Barbie dolls and her
blanket. In my own case it was several pictures of my family
and some underwear and socks in an ugly yellow suitcase next
to my sleeping bag, and other than the clothes that were hanging in the closet, it was all I had. Believe me when I say that

we had almost nothing and yet we were happier than ever. We played, we ate ranch beans with cut up hot dogs in them or fish sticks, we read books and told stories and we talked about their mother. We gave each other love and shared love amongst ourselves in weak moments and we formed the strongest of bonds, bonds that would never again be broken. It was without question, the best time of my life.

I could now start working and making money. The manager at the Chevy dealership was true to his word and when I showed up he gave me a spot just inside the big building, the old Crown Plumbing building. The spot he gave me was right next to the office. It was the spot where new hires were put so that they could be watched by those inside the office. It was no problem for me, I was capable of doing very good work and anxious to prove that I was worth the wait, and since I knew no one there and was desperate for money, working nonstop was not a problem, either.

By the time I received my first paycheck, we were broke. And when I say broke, I mean really flat broke. The night before I got my first paycheck, I had just enough money to go to McDonalds and buy one hamburger. I cut it in half and gave it to the kids. I had to ask them if they had any coffee that was old and going to be thrown away, and if so, could I have a cup. They gave me some. It was a humbling experience and I don't ever want to be in that position again.

Most of the people there were Hispanic and I knew no Spanish at all. Hell, I knew absolutely nothing about Hispanic people. I think that the first ones I had ever met were in Phoenix, but I quickly learned that they have deep religious convictions and they are very hard-working, dependable people.

One of the first people that I got to meet was Phil's younger brother, Ron. He was an insurance adjuster and was there often. There was a body man down at the other end of the shop that appeared to be from the area because he also spoke with a big Southern drawl. I found out that his name was Buford Price. He was tall and thin with a graying beard, and kept to himself most of the time. He kept his distance from me for a long time, but I could tell that he was keeping an eye on me too, as if watching to see if I'd make it or not and what I was made of. I took a liking to Buford because of two things, he kept to himself, much like I did and he liked the same music I did and he wasn't afraid to play it loud. You could tell when Buford was there because "Stairway to Heaven" or "Free Bird" would be blasting from his stall. There were a lot of people there and I kept my distance from all of them, speaking only when spoken to and saying hello or goodbye when I needed to. There were two girls that worked in the office and one of them was Diane. She was a knockout and wore the newest fashions and wore them tight, and it became obvious over time that everyone in the building wanted to sleep with her. I went out of my way not to speak to her any more than I had to, I didn't need the trouble and at the time I was so pissed about Sandy that I avoided as many women as I could. I was convinced that women in general were more grief than they were worth and I needed no part of it. Sandy had left her mark on me and I swore that I would never again marry or be hurt by another woman. I have to say that I was hurting as much from being discarded as I was from still loving her.

As time went on I got to meet each person in the shop, although I minded my own business and waited for them to approach me first. One of the cleanup people was a guy named Tyrone Pickett, from Galveston, Texas. I knew of Galveston from the Glenn Campbell song, but never realized that we were anywhere near it. Tyrone said that it was an island about 55 miles to the south, but there were no jobs to be found there, so he had to drive for hours each day just to work there. He was a great guy and we hit it off instantly. He had this infectious smile and he was such a nice person that you just enjoyed talking to him. He took nothing for granted, appreciating everything he had and everyone he met. And he could make you laugh no matter what kind of bad mood you were in. As time went on, he became engaged to a girl named Gwendolyn and he liked me so much that he invited me to his wedding in Galveston. I hope that they are still together and happy.

There was another porter there, I can't remember his name now and wouldn't put it here even if I did, but he sold all kinds of things on the side, from watches to spray guns to passports to real guns. I asked him one day if he could sell me a phony driver's license and he said that he could get me one but why, he sold real driver's licenses from other states and some of them had no photo on them so they were as good as gold. I bought one and inherited the name that was on it and became Bert Silver. It appeared to be a real license and it didn't expire for a year or two, so if pulled over I could maybe avoid Ohio finding out where we were. After I had the license I made copies of my birth certificate and using white out, inserted my new name and then made more copies. I knew then that I'd make a lousy forger, but it was the best that I could do and better than nothing, in case I ever needed it.

I wrote my first letter to my parents and for the first time used the Bert Silver name and the Boone Road address. In the letter I wrote as if I was an old friend of the family and said that my family was just fine and that I hoped that their family was, too. It let them know where I was and that we were doing well. I told them in a roundabout way that when I felt comfortable enough I would call and say hello and catch up on any news from home.

When I eventually did make that phone call, I did it from a pay phone just to make sure it couldn't be traced because I knew that there were warrants out now for my arrest. I wasn't really sure what I was wanted for, but I knew that they were looking for me because of what had happened in Phoenix and I didn't want to take any chances.

My parents were so happy to hear from me that Mom cried as soon as she heard my voice and then yelled with joy when she heard the voices of Brian and Melissa. It was one of those times that imbeds itself in your memory; it felt so good to talk to them and to put them at ease. We were all right, I was working at a dealership, we had our own apartment and the kids were in a good school. I was beginning to build a circle of people around us, people that didn't know it at the time, but would later be a protective barrier for us. I know all that made my parents feel a lot better. They were very surprised that we were in Texas. Dad mentioned that he would have never guessed that I would go there. The news from up there was interesting too. They said that Sandy had disconnected the phone so that I couldn't call her and beg for forgiveness after I realized that I couldn't handle the distraught kids. Distraught? Not hardly. They weren't even mentioning her name. And raising them was a treasure, not a burden. Sandy was beside herself that I had found the nuts to disappear in the first place and not finding us in Florida had really pissed her off. And then when she found out that they were inches away from catching us in Phoenix but didn't, she was pushed to the point of absolute hatred for me. Mother said that she had read in the paper that Sandy had filed for divorce and custody in Ohio and would surely get everything we owned plus custody of the children and then she laughed hysterically and said, "She'll get legal custody of two kids that she didn't want and can't find."

Dad said that they were going to go to Florida soon to visit my younger brother Jack and his family for Christmas. He said that they needed to get away from the constant pressure up there from the police and Sandy. Sandy had told them that she was sure that they knew where we were and were helping us and that she wanted the police to arrest them and hold them until they spilled the beans. But my parents had strength, more strength than I ever imagined and told everyone that they knew nothing and for that matter, were upset with me for leaving in the first place. And they really hadn't known where we were anyway, until they got that first letter from a man named Bert Silver.

It wasn't at all easy being a single parent, but to this day I believe that it is easier for a single man to raise two kids than it is for a single woman. The reason I say that is because first of all, I had the complete confidence of my children and most of the people that we met and I had an ability to be able to discipline the kids with just the tone of my voice. Secondly, I always had the opportunity to make enough money to pay for everything. It must surely be harder for women who are single parents out there because I believe that in general they make less money and therefore have more of a struggle raising kids alone. Without the money it is harder to get good child care and I'm sure that single mothers must sacrifice more than I ever had to sacrifice to ensure that their children have what they need. Having gone through it myself, I have nothing but praise for all the single women out there raising children with little or no help from the father. And I don't call those people fathers, I call them something else. Anyway, for me the toughest part was being alone so much and always wondering if tomorrow would be the day that we got caught. I wasn't worried about jail really, I knew that the kids had no desire to live with their mother and living with her would not be in their best interest and getting caught would put them right where they didn't need to be. That's what I worried about.

Things were working out just fine at the apartments and we slowly began to make friends. We moved into a two-bedroom apartment right in front of the pool and the couple back at the motel moved into the one-bedroom apartment we moved out of. Chuck and Lori Haynes were further down in the complex and had an even bigger apartment. He was working as a maintenance man and management was starting to find out that he didn't know quite as much as he had said that he did about maintenance, but his desire to learn kept him in the job, just as the desire to find work had got him the job in the first place. He did what any of us would have done when applying for a job that he desperately needed—he had fibbed just a little bit. I didn't blame him; I would have done the same thing had I needed to. They were great people and we helped each other whenever we could. Lori was walking my kids to school each morning and walking them back to her place after school each day, keeping them for me until I could get home. About once a week Lori would have supper ready for all of us. We were bonding with people and they were becoming our family and us theirs.

In general, the kids and I kept to ourselves as much as we could. After getting home from work, I would get the kids from Chuck and Lori and I would sit on the stairs in front of the apartment and watch them play. There were hundreds of kids in the complex, so finding someone to play with was never a problem although they were taught to stay directly in front of our apartment door where I could keep an eye on them at all times. It was a large apartment complex, filled with people from all over the world and it was easy for us to blend in and become invisible.

We weren't in the two-bedroom apartment long when we bought a couple of parakeets to keep us company. I hung the birdcage on a hook in the small dining room and we could watch them play and chatter to each other, it seemed to make us feel whole. Somehow adding the birds made an apartment into a home. In my bedroom I had my sleeping bag laid out unzipped and open on the floor with blankets on top of it. Next to that I had my yellow suitcase, and in it my underwear and socks and every important paper that I had, always ready to make a quick exit if necessary. In the kid's bedroom, they had the two sleeping bags laid out side by side and their little suitcase of favorite things alongside their sleeping bag. As time went on we began to buy things to make life easier for us, but we actually had everything we needed right from the start.

One day I was home from work and I had the kids playing in the living room while I made supper when I heard a knock at the door. As usual, I panicked, thinking it could be the police. Every time someone knocked on the door it was instant panic for us. Who could it be? What should we do? Do we need to grab our most important things and get out? All of those things go through your mind every time. That time it turned out to be two teenagers wearing white shirts and ties. They wanted to talk to me about religion and I proceeded to tell them that I was Catholic and a firm believer in God. I think that I almost had them talked into Catholicism before they left and they applauded my beliefs when they said good-bye. I thanked them for asking about us and got the kids washed up and ready for another one of my famous suppers, macaroni and cheese and spinach. The next evening I came home from work to find a big yellow naughahyde couch on my porch and I stood there for a minute wondering where it could have come from. Then I remembered those two young fellows and I realized that they had seen inside our home and could easily see that we had no furniture of any kind, nothing at all except for the ugly used kitchen table and chairs I had just bought for 20 bucks. The couch came from those two kids, I'm sure of it, but I firmly believe that it was the Lord looking out for us again. He sent those guys to our door. Now not only did we have each other, we had two birds, a kitchen table and a couch.

Notre Dame Catholic Church was just down the street and we started going there every Sunday. It was a very nice church with an upper balcony which was exactly where we chose to sit. We were there, albeit almost invisible, and yet we could thank God and praise him for all of the good that was befalling us. The kids enjoyed being in the balcony and they really liked putting money in the collection basket when it was passed around. I trusted the Catholic faith, a big part of my own heritage, although I still prefer mass in Latin rather than in English. If anyone needed to confess their sins and be appreciative of the words *Dominus Vobiscum*, it was me and each time I did, I asked God to do what was best for my children no matter what.

I was going out of my way to avoid women whenever possible. I don't know if I was just mad at all of them because of the bullshit that I felt came with them or if I felt guilty for having taken the kids from their mother. Maybe I was just so mad at Sandy that I couldn't get over it. Maybe I was still in love with her. But in any store I would always go to the line that had a male at the register if I could, even if it was the longest line. It was just easier for me that way. But then one night a few weeks later I had put the kids to bed and they were already asleep when I got a very faint knock on my door. The door had a peephole so that I could look to see who it was, a prerequisite when you are on the run. You make sure that you have peepholes and an alternate means of escape. It was one of the girls that worked in the office at the apartments. I opened the door and with a big smile she asked me if I had change for a 20 dollar bill for lunch money for her kids. She was wearing a see-through teddy and had her robe draped over one arm, evidently she had taken the robe off just outside my door. I could see that she was not embarrassed about the fact that I could readily see every part of her and I could also tell that she wasn't going to take no for an answer. I let her in.

That night I started to realize that a single man with two children was a curiosity to most women. For some unknown reason women were very curious about me and why it was just me and the two kids. I would learn to use that to our advantage in the years to come.

At work things were going okay. I was proving myself to everyone and the last thing that I wanted to do was disappoint Phil. He had been patient enough to allow me to show up whenever I could after giving me the job on the spot that first day. As I write this, Phil Crosby is living about 25 miles from me and in the fight of his life battling brain cancer. I recently went to see him after his brother, Ron, told me about it. It was the first time in over 20 years that we had seen each other. We laughed as we talked about how he gave me my first chance in Houston although he had very little memory of it. He talked incessantly about his two children. Ron has been a close friend of mine ever since we met way back in 1981. Ron and I have crossed paths a million times since then with my being in the body shop business and him being an adjuster in the car insurance business. Ron is just like his brother Phil: friendly, honest and down to earth and to this day I consider them like brothers.

I was still working in front of the office windows and one day I realized that every time I glanced into the office, Diane would be looking right at me. The more I looked into the office the more I saw her watching me. And the more I saw her watching me, the more I ignored her when I went into the office.

I watched all of the others trying their best to get her attention, sometimes boldly telling her how good she looked that day, other times bluntly asking her if she liked women because she sure as hell didn't seem to like men. She was enough to make their mouths water. I just stayed away from her completely; I didn't need any trouble at work nor did I need the hassle. I'd rather whack off than be put through hell by another woman ever again.

It was almost Christmas of 1981 now and I was trying to buy us the things that we absolutely had to have, but also begin saving money for when I would really need it and I knew that one day we would need it to get out of trouble or get out of town, whichever turned out to be our best option. We never went without what we needed, we just did without everything else. Having too many material things can be a problem when you know you may need to move again and most likely have to leave them behind. And I also knew that one day it would probably take a very good lawyer to keep us together and that wouldn't be cheap. I stopped at a furniture store on my way home one payday and looked at inexpensive bunk beds for the kids. They had some that were perfect, just the right size for the room and they looked pretty darned good too, so I bought them and paid them to deliver. It ate up most of our cash for a week or two, but it was well worth getting those beds for them to sleep in and it made the place much more like home.

The kids asked me one night if we were going to get a Christmas tree and I told them that I didn't think we should this year, we had each other and Santa didn't care if we had a tree or not. The truth was that I had enough money to buy a tree, but not enough to buy anything to put on it if we did buy one. But then I realized that we needed as many of the normal parts of our lives that we could get and having a Christmas tree was an important part of a child's Christmas and besides, if I didn't buy a tree it would be the first Christmas in their lives that they didn't have one, so I decided to get the smallest and cheapest one that we could find. We walked up to the corner of Bellaire and Boone where they were selling Christmas trees and I picked out a tree from the back of the tent, the ones that were already losing needles and had seen better days. I showed it to the kids and they took me straight to a much nicer tree down a few rows and at that point I had to tell them that the one I picked out would be just the right size for our apartment. I just couldn't afford the one that they had picked out.

One of the men working there must have overheard us talking or maybe he saw the disappointment in their faces, I don't know, but when we took our little tree up to the counter to pay for it, he said, "This tree is four dollars, do you have four dollars?" I answered with a "Yes, I do," and then he said, "Well the one your kids showed you also happens to be four dollars today, now which one do you want?" I looked at him confused and he patted me on the shoulder and said, "It's Christmas for Christ's sake, Merry Christmas from me!"

It was because of people like him and Phil Crosby and the kids with the couch, people like the Dempsey and Weaver families and the Jerry Smiths and the John Moore's and John Lewis's and the Haynes's family and on and on that we made it. It was God that put us on a course to follow, and it was his plan that we meet these people. These exact people! These are the people that gave me the help and the desire to succeed and to be the best father that these two children could ever have. I needed to make these people proud and I needed to thank them, to thank them by proving to all of them that I was not making a big mistake and neither were they by helping us. And if it hadn't been these people, it would have been other people just like them. All of these people, from the family that helped us with the welding, to the Haynes family that made us a part of their family, these people showed us a kindness that we had never known before. We found out during these years that the world is full of good people that are willing to help without question and sometimes without regard for themselves. It is an amazing fact that we learned every time we turned around on this amazing journey.

Christmas came and went and I was back at work and then one day I was standing up in the middle of a car that I had just cut the roof off of when I heard someone behind me call my name. I recognized the voice and it just didn't compute. I was stunned. It was my father's voice. He was standing right there next to the car. They were on their way back from spending Christmas in Florida and they had decided to head west instead of north and surprise us. And what a surprise it was! I cried right there in front of everybody when we hugged. I can't explain how good it felt to see someone from my family after all that we had been through. We walked around to the front of the dealership and mother was waiting in the motor home. It just doesn't get any better than that. She started crying the second she saw me. After introducing them to Phil Crosby I left work and had them follow me to our apartment and we waited for school to let out. When it did, Mom, Dad and I were there to meet the kids and what a happy sight it was for all of us. I had never seen them happier; the only time that even came close was when I told them that they did not have to ever go back. And so we had our second Christmas in less than two weeks! My father gave me a used Kenwood receiver that he had brought from my brother Jack and it became our first piece of electronic entertainment. Now we could listen to music—damn, it just kept getting better. I still have that Kenwood receiver upstairs in the attic. I'll keep it as long as I live. The memories of lying on the floor after the kids were asleep and listening to it mean way too much to me to ever let it go.

The kids and I took my parents to Notre Dame Church that Sunday and for my father it was probably the first time he had been inside of a church since the wine in the water fiasco when I was a child. Seeing us and realizing just how happy we were had put their minds at complete rest for the first time since we had left, and all of us had very good reason to thank God.

My parents stayed as long as they could without arousing too much suspicion up in Pennsylvania. But the day did come when they had to leave and they waited until after they had walked the kids to school and after I had gone to work before they did. Talk about a sad time, I remember coming home that night to a goodbye note that they had left on the kitchen table, with a "see you later" from Dad written on it, and so it was just the three of us again. It was a sad couple of days until we recovered and got on with our lives once again. Mother told me later that after their trip down to see us, Dad had said that for the first time, he firmly agreed that what I had done was in fact the right thing and he never wavered or doubted it again.

Hiding in Houston in 1982.

CHAPTER NINE:
A New Life Blooms

The holidays were over; it was 1982 now and we were settling into our new lives. The kids were always doing something at school, whether it was a play or a musical and I was always there. I wouldn't have missed it for the world. I was such a big part of their lives and they were my whole life and nothing else really mattered. If they had something going on, we were going. By then the teachers at Chancellor were probably beginning to figure out our story, but they had also seen the love that we had for each other and the happiness that we shared amongst the three of us. They may not have known the whole story, but they knew right from wrong and they knew that what we had was right, even if it was illegal. Teachers have an innate sense about them that I liken to animals. An animal can tell quickly who to love and who to fear, they just know. And teachers can spot sincerity like an eagle sees a mouse.

We were making more and more friends at the apartments and we were actually beginning to accumulate material things. One day I decided that it was time for us to get a television. For the first time in my life I went to a pawnshop and bought a used TV, a sharp 19-inch color beauty for a hundred bucks. It reminded me of the one I had pawned almost 10 years earlier. It's funny how something so insignificant can bring you back to a different place and time. I cried for her that night. I cried for all four of us that night.

I sought out a psychiatrist that would talk to the kids and

make sure that they were all right with this whole thing. The last thing I wanted to do was harm them and if I was, I needed to know so that I could take a different course. The best of the best was a Dr. Morton Katz and I found out quickly that these people do not work cheap. I would bring the kids to see him about once a month and he would talk to them sometimes together, sometimes separately depending on what he felt was best. Sometimes he would want to talk to me alone. He always talked to me after each meeting with the kids anyway, just to keep me in the loop.

It was an expensive undertaking, but if what I had done was doing more damage than good to the kids, I would have given them up. This went on for about six months, and in the opinion of the doctor, the kids were where they wanted to be and doing just fine. That kind of reassurance is worth any amount of money.

A young couple had just moved in above us, Jere' and Don and their son Eric, and Eric began showing up in our apartment whenever he wanted to. He was about three years old and would just walk out of their apartment, come down the steps and just walk right into our place. We got to know them pretty well because of this strange event. It was almost as if he felt like our home was his. Every time they turned around upstairs, he would come down to play with my kids. There was also little Theresa riding around the apartments on her red tricycle all the time. Everywhere you went you would see her, just riding around all over the place and smiling at everyone. She was a free spirit and would go wherever she chose to and then after a while you would see Sydney or Kelly come walking past looking for her.

Remember the guy I told you about meeting back at the motel? The one whose girlfriend was a dancer? Well, they had moved into the one-bedroom apartment after we moved out and into our two-bedroom. I can't remember his name, but he came over and knocked on my door shortly after they moved in and wanted to thank me for telling them about the apartments and for talking to him back at the motel when others wouldn't. He asked me to come over to their apartment one night for a glass of wine, his way of thanking me he said, and he wouldn't take no for an answer. So we agreed on a night and time and I asked Jere' if she would baby sit for a little while that night and she was more than happy to earn some money because they, like all of the rest of us, were always broke. That night I walked over to the one bedroom apartment that used to be ours and his girlfriend answered the door and let me in. You could tell that she had been drinking and she immediately started kissing me. And then she slowly took my hands and placed them on her breasts and her butt. I was in a state of shock. "What was going on here? Where is the guy that invited me over? What is this?" I asked her.

They had just moved in and had about as much furniture as we did, which was almost none. But they had throw pillows on the floor and she pulled me down onto them, again, putting my hands on her breasts and undoing my shirt. "Where is he?" I asked again. "He's here, have some wine," she said. She kept kissing me and began undoing my zipper, and I was trying to get up and go toward the door when she said, "Please don't go, he'll be mad at both of us." "What the hell are you talking about," I said, "if he walks in he's going to kill us both."

"He is in the closet and he likes to watch me with people that he likes, and he thinks a lot of you," she whispered as she chewed on my ear. "I'm fixin' to make you very happy and all three of us are gonna enjoy it," she said, as her dress fell to the floor and exposed a very beautiful body.

I didn't know what to do, this being my first and only experience with that kind of thing. Was he going to come out and hit me with a hammer or did he really get off watching this kind of thing? None of that really mattered anyway, because I was so confused and nervous that getting it up would have been beyond impossible. I stood up, adjusted my clothes, apologized to the both of them and hit the door as fast as I could. For years I wondered about that night. Was he mad at her because I had left? After that, I seldom saw them and they kept their distance from me for reasons known only to them. Their two redheaded daughters would come over once in a while, usually asking for something to eat. One day they showed up and made the three of us laugh uncontrollably because the first thing they said was, "Y'all got any breeaadd?" in a very Cajun accent. It was so funny that it cracked us up. We gave them our loaf of bread. I'm sorry that I offended them, whoever they were and I don't regret meeting them and their redheaded girls—they were a trip. They made us laugh every time they came to visit us, and that was usually right about supper time.

Things were okay at work and I was slowly making more friends. One day Buford, the older fellow down at the other end of the shop, came up to me and asked me if I wanted to go with him to get a soda water. It was the first time that he had acknowledged me other than the normal obligatory hello's when we passed each other. I wondered if my probationary period with him was over, maybe he was going to accept me after all. I didn't want to hurt his feelings, but I had no desire to drink soda water, whatever it was. I told him that I didn't care for any soda water, but that I'd go with him anyway. As it turned out, he bought a Coke and I bought a Mountain Dew. He said "I thought you didn't want one," and I told him that I didn't know what a soda water was until he bought one. We called it pop up north, I told him. Buford laughed his ass off. "Damn Yankees," he said, "you don't know what the hell to call anything, but you're here and we're stuck with y'all." From that day on Buford and I hit it off and he nicknamed me "the damned Yankee." I used to tell him that Virginia wasn't that far from Gettysburg and that he was probably a damn Yankee too. That's when he changed my nickname to "damn Yankee ass-hole." We wound up best friends and still see each other today. Years later he would go on to fight his own battle with cancer, and luckily, he would win.

I also met Claire Monahan and Jeffrey Glaser at Courtesy Chevrolet. They both worked in different departments of the dealership and both lived near me and so we decided to ride together and save gas. I would drive to Jeff's apartment, park my car and ride with him and then we would pick up Claire on the way. We all saved money because we just gave Jeff gas money each week and it worked out well for all of us. Jeff was infatuated with Claire and she was all he talked about when-ever we were alone. I can't blame him; she was good looking, smart, had a great body and a great attitude. If I had been in the market, I would have fought him for her.

I saw a lot of people come and go while I was there and I had a soft spot for new people coming in from out of state. One of them was a crazy guy from Boston that started not too long after I did, his name was Kevin Hayes. He was the kind of guy that you like the very second you meet him, easygoing, nonintrusive and he had a unique sense of humor. He would become one of my closest friends. They put Kevin outside the main shop in a smaller building where he could do his spe-cialty, fiberglass work, and not bother anyone else with the itching and the rashes that go along with it. After Kevin and I became friends I asked if I could move out to the smaller shop with Kevin, and Phil said okay. We got to know each other well and we had a lot of fun together. Buford, Kevin and myself, what a crew we became. If anyone had problems with anything, the others would help get things done. We made a good team together and there was nothing that we couldn't do. One day Kevin and I walked into the main building for coffee and there was Buford, yelling at everyone to be quiet while Phil Collins' "I can feel it comin' in the air tonight, hold on," blared from his stereo. Another morning we got together for our morning cup of coffee and Kevin was telling us a story about something and with a cigarette and his coffee in the same hand, he brought his hand up to his mouth and confused about what he meant to do, spilled his coffee all down the front of his shirt when he put the cigarette to his mouth. After that we started calling him Pigpen. He was always covered in dirt from all that fiberglass work that he did and his stall was always a mess. But he was the Corvette man and since the rest of us didn't want anything to do with fiberglass work, Kevin always stayed busy with every 'vette that came in. He called it job security.

So there we were, the damn Yankee, Pigpen and the old redneck, Buford. Every time he called me a Yankee I would remind him of how close Virginia was to Pennsylvania. That's when he would start swearing and raising hell. "Oh, Hell no, I ain't no damn Yankee, you asshole," he would say.

1982 was going by without any big problems. My sister, Linda, her husband, Mike, and their son, Chris, came down that year. Chris was a few years younger than my kids were and so we told him that we were in Alaska. That way if anyone asked him later and he did slip up and tell them he had seen us, he would say that we're in Alaska. Each time someone from my family came to see us it was always a real treat for us. But when it was time for them to leave it was awful, there is no other word for it. The pain of being alone again always took a while to go away, but over time it always did.

One day the school called me at work and told me that

Melissa was sick, she had a nosebleed and was running a fever and they said that it could be serious. I called Jere' and had her go get Melissa from school and I left work. By the time I got home her fever was 103 degrees and I called on our friends for help. They said to put her in a tub of cold water and see if you could control the fever. My little girl screamed her lungs out as I forced her into the ice cold water. It was hell, you know the feeling, you've probably had to do it yourself before with one of your own children. I wound up taking her to the old Alief hospital on Bellaire that night and they immediately admitted her. She had quite an infection, viral syndrome is what they called it and she wound up in the hospital for three days; Brian and I were almost always with her. That's when we met Dr. Phillip Bellan, the attending doctor. As he told us her status and that she would be all right, he asked me when she had broken her collarbone. I told him that I was unaware that she ever had and he showed all three of us the X-ray. It clearly showed a mended fracture of her collarbone. My guess is that it happened when she fell out of the bunk in the camper in Phoenix. She never complained once about it, what a trooper she was, heck, they both were. Not long afterwards Brian fell from Jere's balcony above us and landed on the handlebars of Don's motorcycle that he parked in front of our porch and next to the stairs. That happened just before I got home from work one day and Jere' had taken him to the emergency room right away. I met up with them at the hospital and all he needed was some stitches in his head and he had a few bruises. Thank God. It could have been much worse. I had visions of a handlebar puncture to the stomach.

Kevin, Buford and I were becoming good friends now and we started going to lunch together a couple of times a week. The closest place was a Denny's restaurant just up the road and one day they decided that I needed to get laid, so they started shopping for a girl for me. They picked out a nice-looking waitress and when she came past our table, they pointed at me and asked her if she knew anyone that would go out with me. They said that I was a nice guy and that they needed to find me a nice girl because I needed some company. Completely embarrassed, I denied all of it and told her not to listen to them. I told her that I was an asshole and she smiled and left.

One day the following week, the three of us were there again and that waitress came up and asked them if they had found me a girl friend yet. Kevin got a great big grin on his face and said, "No, have you?" She walked away and bussed a couple of tables, came back and looked right at Kevin and said, "He doesn't look too bad; I guess I could help y'all out. I have an eight-month-old daughter and I'm alone. He doesn't look like a killer to me. I wouldn't mind if he wouldn't." I was humiliated by now, my face red as it always gets when I'm embarrassed. I couldn't wait to get out of there. The next day she called Kevin at work and without telling me, he gave her our address.

She showed up at our apartment soon after. Her name was Becky and she said that she needed to get laid just as bad as she figured I did, so we'd get along just fine. She had driven over to see if I was legitimate about being a single parent. She was the kind that needed material things and spending some quality time on my sleeping bag that night probably didn't impress her. But she came over several times after that and one time she even made supper for us, down home country fried steak, potatoes and fried okra topped off with cornbread (something I never acquired a taste for). She was from Junction, Texas, so she knew what home cooking was all about, she said. I had never heard of okra before and really didn't care for it but I told her it was great. And so we had a fling for awhile, usually just sex and a shower at her apartment during my lunch hour and on her days off or at our place after the kids were asleep. My kids were certainly not her favorite things, money and sex were.

It didn't last very long; Becky came over one evening and was making supper for us when she saw Melissa reaching into her purse. She started screaming at her like she had done something terrible. I asked her to keep her voice down and not panic, but she freaked out. "No one gets in my purse," she said. I told her that my daughter was only seven and just a kid and hadn't even seen a purse in a long time and that she would never take anything from it, she was just curious. Becky lived and breathed for her tip money and it was her tip money in the purse that got her so wound up. She never forgave my daughter for it and I never forgave Becky for how she screamed at my daughter. I will say that it was the last time that Melissa ever got into someone's purse. It was also the last time she would ever be welcome at our home.

Becky came over to see me at work trying to make up one day. Sometimes she would call and say she needed me, but I told her to stop calling and I let it go. She never realized that at the time I held so little regard for women at all, certainly not one that could lose it over something as insignificant as that. Then she started calling Kevin at work, trying to get him to help her get us back together, saying that it would be the right thing since he was the one that got us together in the first place. One day he said, "Schulz, she won't stop calling me now." I told him that it served him right for setting us up in the first place, but then he said that she was starting to call him at home and that would get him in big trouble. Kevin was one of the most happily married people that I had ever met with Christine and little Kevin and Dylan at home. I told him that I would talk to her and stop all of that and so I drove over to the diner and talked to her. It got ugly when I asked her to never call Kevin or me again. I didn't need a woman in the first place and definitely not one with a temper like hers. And so, it was over for us, she was the kind of woman any man would want to settle down with except that I wasn't looking to settle down and I had a firm dislike for anyone who tried to get between me and my kids, not to mention that I could hold a grudge a hell of a long time.

It was a good year for us. We were really making friends now and I was slowly cocooning us in a circle of support, always aware that there would be a day of reckoning and it could come any day, maybe tomorrow. We had new friends next door to us, Carol Collins and her daughter, Angela, Carol's brother, Jim, and their mother, James. Yes, her name really was James. They became close allies and helped me take good care of my kids. If we needed to be fed, they would feed us; if they needed to be fed we did that. If I needed someone to watch the kids, they would do it. They had faith in me and they trusted me, and so I entrusted them to watch my kids when necessary. I had told them enough of the story that if anything were to happen they would do whatever they needed to do to hide the kids until I could get them.

I was lying on the floor underneath a pickup truck one day at work putting the bed back in place after the paint work was finished and I heard someone call my name. It was Diane; she was crouched down on bent knees at the side of the truck. She had a skirt on and it was obvious that she was not wearing any panties. She said that she hadn't seen the kids since the day that I had applied for a job and she wanted to see them again and find out how we were doing. She asked me if she could come to our apartment and if I would draw her a map. Yeah, right. It wasn't hard to figure out what she wanted. So, thinking with the wrong head, I drew her a map. She showed up that night right about eight o'clock as I was doing the dishes and the kids were watching television. The kids remembered her from when I had applied for the job. She helped me read stories to the kids and get them into bed and then, after they were asleep, I took her to my sleeping bag. She proceeded to teach me things that I had never even heard of. I'm not complaining, but we got almost no sleep that night and we still went to work the next morning.

Things started changing at work almost immediately. Diane would come out to my stall several times a day and want to talk or go to lunch. It didn't take long for the other guys to get a little jealous of the whole thing. Most of them had been trying their best to sleep with her and I hadn't even been talking to her unless I had to and now all of a sudden I was the chosen one. The guys started to make fun of me and they began teasing her and that started the ball rolling. It was beginning to get complicated and I hated complications, I didn't need the crap and I was trying to encircle us with friends, not alienate people. Diane was coming over about three times a week now; she even brought her mother one night. They were both drunk and Diane asked me if I would sleep with her mother. Now, I had been through some crazy things back up north in years gone by and I had learned some crazy things in Houston already, but this was just not going to happen. I declined as graciously as I possibly could.

One day at work something happened between Diane and Phil, and she came flying out of the office just cussing up a storm. Phil had told her that one of the rules there was that she could not be involved with another employee and she was furious. She told me that for her to see me she would have to quit and so I told her to just calm down and that we should just put things on the back burner for awhile and see what happened. She evidently thought that we had more between us than I thought we had and she really blew her lid. She was yelling at me in front of everyone saying that she was willing to quit for me and that she would move in with us at the apartment if I wanted her to. "Make a decision," she told me. I did. I walked away.

After that things were never the same between her and me, nor would they be the same between Phil and me. It was stupid, I never wanted to get involved anyway and now it was affecting my job. I just had a hard time saying no to women that wanted me. Maybe I needed them to want me after my wife didn't. Maybe I was just getting even, I don't know.

There was another new guy in the shop now, Homer Kovacs, and he had recently come to town from Florida. He wasn't at the shop long before he saw that I had some problems with Phil and Diane and he said that his older brother was the manager of an independent body shop almost across the street from the Motel 6 that we had stayed at when we first moved to Houston. His brother was looking for good body men and he was paying more per hour. Homer said that he couldn't work for his brother without it causing ill feelings between them and he didn't want that. One day Kevin and I drove over there at lunch and talked to his brother, Jimmy, and he did manage the shop and did need help. The shop was called Car Craft and it was much smaller than I expected. It was a whole lot closer to where I lived and it did pay more, so Kevin and I both agreed to go to work for him although out of respect for Phil, we would come one at a time. I would go first. I could solve several problems at once by leaving Courtesy. I could put Diane, Becky and Phil behind me and be closer to home as well. And if it worked out like we hoped that it would, Kevin would follow a month later and we would both be making more money.

I gave two weeks notice to Phil and when the time came I said my goodbyes, thanked Phil for all his help, packed my tools and moved in at Car Craft. It was a tiny shop compared to Courtesy and it had outdated equipment in it, but it would become more than a job to me. The address was 9703b Plainfield, I'll never forget it. It really was almost right across the street from the Motel 6 that the kids and I stayed at when we first came to town. It was and still is painted orange and stands out as you go by. I know because I go by often, just to remember. I think it's good to remember where you came from and how you got to where you are.

The owner was a man named Mike Milner, a tall slender man and you could tell that he was used to the finer things in life just by talking to him. He had a gorgeous blond for a girl-friend and he always had a corvette, always. Jimmy was the manager, a short stocky redneck fellow with a unique laugh that automatically made others laugh with him. Jimmy was from Alabama or Georgia, I can't remember which, and he liked to wear cowboy boots and a cowboy hat all the time. He turned out to be a real nice guy; he would help anyone who needed help if he saw that they were in turn willing to help others. The first thing Jimmy asked me as I unloaded my tools was, "Do you know anything about Nissan 240ZXs?" "Never worked on one before," I said, "but I'm not afraid of them either." "Good," he said, "we have four of them here with nothing in front of the dash, frame rails cut off, sheet metal gone and the motors hanging from chains, I hope you're ready to make some money." I was. And I told him so. Then I began to prove it to him.

The shop had two painters, a guy named Danny and another painter named Jeff Stephens. They also had two body man's helpers, both Vietnamese. Their names were To and Hahn. Jimmy said that they were very hard-working guys, but they needed to be taught direction and finesse. They did not have one body man, not one. They had quit when they heard more body men were coming. Us body men are greedy bas-tards, even if we can't do all the work in the shop, we still want it all. We don't want anyone else to get it because a wrecked car to a body man is money in the bank. A body man will survey a parking lot full of wrecked cars and all he'll see is money and he will want it all. It's our nature, just like praying for rain, it fills the shops up. Anyway, I got the silent treatment from almost everyone there until I proved myself, again. We always have to prove ourselves everywhere we go. The painters wouldn't talk to me because they blamed me for the loss of their friends that quit. Go figure. Once To and Hahn saw what I could do, they quickly jumped in and helped me and between us we cleaned up the place, getting rid of all the old jobs and then cleaning the shop up so that we wouldn't have to feel shitty about coming to work in a nasty, dirty little shop.

Back at home, the kids were doing great in school. From time to time they would take these assessment tests and both would score above grade level in almost every category. Brian would have stars going all the way off the sheet. We could not have chosen a better school for the children. The principal and several of the teachers knew me pretty well now and helped me in more ways than one. The ability that these people had to read between the lines and assist parents like myself was well beyond what they were paid to do and yet they made the world a better place by going above and beyond each and every day. We were comfortable now, surrounded by friends, encircled like a spider in the center of her nest. Some were aware of our situation, some completely oblivious. Like a chess set, I had prepared for my inevitable battle. But unlike Sandy, instead of using the children as chess pieces, I was using people around us instead. I was looking beyond the next move and plotting a way out of an eventual checkmate. The kids were growing fast and Sandy was missing so much. I would justify her loss by thinking that we were a family with her, and we are a family without her. It had been her choice.

We made it a habit to open the door of the dining room closet and with a pencil and yardstick, I would measure both of the kids on the inside of the door. It was my way of showing them and reminding myself of just how fast they were growing. If I didn't feel like cooking, I would take them to Grandys where we could get a good meal and they could play on the playground equipment while I drank coffee and watched them play themselves out of energy. I would sometimes have to carry them both from the car to their beds, because they would conk out on the way home. We had Jere' above us, Carol and Jimmy Collins next to us, Chuck and Lori down the way and a pool just in front of the door of the apartment. We swam a lot. If there was one thing I did well, it was teaching them both how to swim. We all loved the water. One day I was swimming with them and soon we had a boatload of kids there. I wondered where all of their parents were because I wound up being the lifeguard for all of them. I was showing off about diving and I showed them what I call a sailor's dive, head first, without your arms above your head. I dove in and hit the bottom of the pool with my head. When I came up I had blood running down my face and all the kids panicked, but not me, I calmly told them that it wasn't as bad as it looked, the water was just making it look worse than it was. I sent Brian to the apartment to get a towel so that I could cover it up and calm all the kids down. I remember walking back to the apartment holding a towel to the side of my head that afternoon. Later that night I went and got a few stitches put in.

There was a groundskeeper that worked there named Aries, an older Hispanic man that picked up papers and trash in return for discounted rent. Aries would always come by on Saturday or Sunday mornings and have coffee with me. He always wanted a cigarette too. Over time he learned that I usually baked on Saturdays and so Sunday mornings became the norm. I liked baking cookies and cupcakes for the kids and tried to always have something for them. It was nice because he spoke no English and I spoke no Spanish, so we spoke by hand gestures. We would have coffee and a few of my world famous molasses cookies and a smoke together on those mornings with basically nothing spoken between us, but we respected each other and that is what made it so nice. Those memories stand out now because they were proof to me that language isn't that important, getting along is more than words, it's trust, respect and friendliness.

I was listening to the radio one night after the kids were asleep and Jere' came down and lightly tapped on the door. With everyone asleep upstairs, she said that she was bored. She didn't work and Don was very domineering, so her quiet time was when everyone was sleeping. She just wanted someone to talk to. Other than her family, she had no life of her own and it made me think of Sandy for the first time in a good while. We had a good time talking that night, staying up way too late, but getting to know each other much better. Over time it became common for her to come downstairs after everyone was asleep and we would talk and play cards. She was strikingly pretty, maybe six or seven years younger than I and she would usually come down after her shower, her hair wet because she didn't dare use her hair drier and make any noise. She didn't want to wake up Don or her two children.

Once in a while she would be pretty depressed about something when I saw her, and one evening I asked her about it and she wouldn't say anything, she just started crying. I suspected that she was in the same situation that Sandy had been in, unhappy and confused, but she never admitted it. Don never hid the fact that he talked to her like she was a servant and yelled at her if anything made him upset and I could tell that it hurt her. As she cried I held her and showed her what it was like to be in the arms of someone who cared, something she desperately needed. She even asked me one night if she and Eric and Kristen could leave with us if we ever had to take off again. I encouraged her to leave him and give herself a chance to be happy in life although I knew that doing so would put Don in the same boat that I had been put it. After that she would come down whenever she needed to talk. And then she started to come down more and more and we usually played cards until midnight or so, she knew when to be back upstairs. I spent many a night just hoping that she would come down, and once in a while she did. Sometimes she just wanted to relax and talk. Other times she needed me to hold her. It didn't take long before I wanted more. And over time, so did she. I learned to know what she wanted on any given night by whether she kissed me or not. If she did, she wanted me to hold her. If she didn't, she just wanted to talk; either way was fine with me. She was such a nice person that just holding her in the peace and quiet and enjoying the smell of her wet, freshly shampooed hair was enough to make me happy. I knew that it made her happy too and although I never told her this, each time that she came down I wished that she never had to leave.

At the shop I was making better money than I ever had in my life, 50 percent of the labor money of every car I repaired. The more you work, the more you make and since I had few friends there at first, I spent a lot of time working, heck, we needed the money anyway and any day we could be found and if anything could help us, it would be money. I was taking home about a grand a week at the time, stashing much of it in my car. I didn't use banks because you can get found that way and I couldn't keep it in the apartment either, if I ever got home and the law was there, I wouldn't be able to get to it. It would be hard to leave town if I couldn't get to our money.

By the time Kevin came over with me, I had made a friend

in Jeff, the painter. Danny, the other painter had quit over some dispute with management. The harder I worked the more money I made and the more cars I put into the paint shop. The more cars I put into the paint shop, the more money Jeff made. He was making better money than he had in a very long time and so was I.

At first he did not talk to me unless it involved a car in the shop, and then one day he asked me to lunch. It was one of those defining moments, you know what I mean? I had been accepted once again. We became good friends after that, friends to the end. Jeff started coming over to the apartment once in a while and he would bring his girlfriend, Carol, with him. She was a good-looking girl with a taste for nice things; you could tell by the way she dressed. They fought a lot and one always seemed to be mad at the other. They eventually split up and he moved back to Georgia and Carol to Florida. Anyway, when Kevin started at the shop Jeff told him, "any friend of Glen's is a friend of mine," and the three of us were a team from then on. With Kevin there I made less money because now there were two body men and enough work for both, but I had been doing the work of two and making the money of two. We worked hard when we worked and we laughed a lot together when we played. There was a restaurant right across the street called, "Slice of Life Pizza" and we usually walked over there for lunch because pizza has always been my favorite food of all time. The work rules were lax and we would stay there way too long, and making matters worse we would sometimes drink beer with our pizza. Sometimes Buford came to visit and would have lunch with us. We had a blast for awhile until one day Jimmy had to come get us. He took our keys and made us sit in his office and drink coffee until he felt that we were all right to drive and then let us go home. He said that if we didn't promise him right then that we would not do that again, he would fire us on the spot. We promised, and we didn't.

That shop was making more profit than it ever had and it was because of us, the three misfits. The Vietnamese guys that worked there were learning a lot from us, they were very hard workers and eager to learn something new each day. With Kevin and I knocking out cars with the help of To and Hahn and Jeff painting them as fast as he could, that shop was rocking. Sometimes we all spent lunch together sitting on five-gallon buckets turned upside down, just sitting in the opening of the shop door, too busy to go eat. One time To saw a rat running towards the dumpster and chased it until he caught it, snapping its neck like a chicken's. He said that they were good eating when it's all you have. I believed him; he had come over from Vietnam in 1977 by floating on a large raft with many others. He used to tell us horrible stories about it.

Things were busy at work but because they were making more money than they had been, they started spending more and more and before long they started to have money flow problems and they had to find a financial backer, a silent partner. They did, but he insisted on having someone that he could trust in the mix, a girl in the office to keep track of the money. Her name was Linda Yokem, and she would change my world. Linda was tall, maybe five-foot-six, thin, pretty and with a heck of a body to go along with the looks. She became the brains of the whole operation and the one everybody wanted to be around. She had a persona that implied that you had a chance to sleep with her and she used it to our advantage with wrecker drivers. They thought that they would get some if they made her happy and the best way to make her happy was to keep bringing wrecked cars; each time being another opportunity to make time with her. It was working well, we were very busy and we were all making money. I don't believe any wrecker driver ever got in her pants, but it was a heck of a carrot dangling in front of them, and it was good for all of us. She knew what she had and she knew how to use it with all of us, and yet to my knowledge, no one ever slept with her.

Sometime in late fall of 1982 someone stole the license plates off of about 20 cars parked at the apartments one night, mine included. No big deal if you're registered in Texas, I wasn't, mine were Arizona plates and Texas knew nothing about my car. The only option I had was to register the car in Texas, which would substantially increase the risk of being found, or leave the car where it was. I chose the latter. The car sat there in the parking lot with no plates until they made me tow it to the body shop and the kids and I walked to wherever we needed to go if we couldn't find a ride. I can remember the many times we walked to Notre Dame church and were all sweaty and tired by the time we got there.

Kevin began picking me up every morning and we would go straight to the Shipley's donuts shop down the street for a coffee and two donuts, my treat. We'd say hi to Gene, the owner, and then go on to work. And every evening he brought me home. This went on for a long time. If we needed anything else I would either ask someone close to me—which I was too proud to do unless it was an emergency—or we would just walk. Walking to the grocery store was no big deal; it was only about a half a mile away, walking back was the hard part. I carried the heavy stuff and the kids walked along in front of me carrying the lighter stuff and complaining the whole way about how heavy it was.

We spent a lot of time at home for a while simply because we had to. It was better than taking the risks that went along with getting new plates. After work I would always sit on the steps in front of the door to our apartment and I would watch the kids play. I would often think about their mother, first remembering how much I had loved her and then thinking about how much of their lives that she was missing. I felt bad for her. But I couldn't imagine not being in their lives, and Sandy had already tried to do that. The steps were the perfect vantage point for watching all directions and I became a staple out there, sitting, smoking, drinking coffee, thinking and watching. I made a lot of friends that way and most of the time others would sit down with me and before long we would have a group, all of us talking about whatever we felt like talking about that day. And all the while I was always quietly watching and planning a way out if they were to show up for us.

I seldom turned the air-conditioning on in the apartment, it was expensive and I was really trying to save money for what would eventually happen. I would usually just leave the front door open while I sat out on the steps. Leaving the door open allowed a breeze and could possibly allow the three of us a fast disappearance if necessary.

I would sometimes just sit on the steps out front in the peace and quiet after the kids were asleep, thinking about their mother, thinking about the life that we used to have and comparing it to the lives that we had now. In years past I would occasionally go through these periods of disappointment. I don't like to call them periods of depression because they weren't, I would just get this blue feeling and an accompanying feeling of disappointment about things. These would always pass with time and then one day they would just return. I can't explain it, but I realized that I had not felt it once since we had left, and I never have since. I think now that it was a reaction to the demeaning way that Sandy talked to me and our leaving changed that.

FBI arrests Glen here in 1983.

CHAPTER TEN:
MEET THE F.B.I.

I was sitting on the steps as I usually did one evening and this girl that lived down a few doors from me started down the sidewalk, coming home from work. We had seen each other many times and it was always a brief hello, how are ya' kind of thing. I wasn't really looking for anyone; I was doing just fine as I was. As she approached the steps she stopped and said hello as was our custom, but then in a real Southern drawl, she said, "It was so hot today, I just wanted to take my clothes off." That got my attention. I hardly knew this woman and I didn't know just what to say other than yes, it was real hot today. She introduced herself, something she had not done before. Her name was Rhonda and she was a single parent with two boys. She was a good-looking woman a few years younger than me and they lived upstairs in the next apartment building.

After all the niceties were over and she walked on to her apartment, I sat there and tried to envision her walking around naked all day and I decided to ask her and the kids over for dinner one night. I'd cook something Yankee style and impress her. Now that I had thought about it, I wanted to see her walk around naked.

We started slowly, talking about my kids and then talking about her two boys. She was a superb mother to the boys and it showed right away. She was from Rosenberg, a small town south of Houston and she had been born and raised there. We wound up having dinner together the next night at her apartment, my kids, her kids and the two of us. She took a liking to my kids immediately and me to hers. My kids took a liking to her quickly, too. It wasn't long before they started asking if they could go over to Rhonda's house while I cleaned.

Rhonda and I got along extremely well. She treated my kids as if they were hers and vice versa, her boys, my son and I would play football, fly kites, throw a baseball around, all the things a normal father does. Rhonda seemed to fit perfectly into the role of surrogate mother to Melissa, showing her all of the feminine things a young girl needs to see, as I was unable to do so. When she had to give the kids to their father for visitation, she would just stay at our place, helping me with whatever needed done.

She absolutely loved children and worked at a day care center, but she did not make a lot of money and so they didn't have any more than we did. It's not that I didn't want to have more, but because of the expense of the lawyer that I knew I would need one day and the fear of having to move on short notice, if any, I didn't spend a lot on extras. Getting caught one day was like death, inevitable, and I knew that good lawyers don't work cheap. Out of the blue one day she came to see me and started crying. She told me that she was moving back in with her mother in Rosenberg. She just couldn't keep up with things, she said, the boys were getting older and needed more and more and money was getting tighter, it would just be best if she moved in with her mother and cared for her and saved some money at the same time. So they moved about 30 miles away and she would pick us up and drive us out there about once a week or so to see them and on weekends when she didn't have the kids, she would come over and stay with us. It was a perfect arrangement, a good woman coming over every other weekend, a woman around us that loved my children as much as she loved me.

We were on the way back from seeing her in Rosenberg one day when the police pulled us over. I had a brake light out on the car, they said. I knew I might be in trouble because I had taken the license plates from Rhonda's old car that didn't run and had put them on my Impala. They weren't stolen, but they did not belong to my car. Anyway, I was pulled over on Highway 90, almost exactly where the movie the *Sugar Land Express* had been filmed years ago. For a second I thought about taking off, but the kids were with me and I would never endanger them. The police officer asked for my driver's license and I gave him my Bert Silver license from New York, now expired. I had not realized it was expired because I seldom ever drove anywhere and always paid cash for everything, you don't need to pull out your driver's license when you are paying cash and so I never noticed. No bank accounts, no checkbooks, no credit cards, nothing on paper that could draw the attention of anyone. That's what you have to do when you're in hiding.

He gave me a warning after I explained that it was not my car, it belonged to my girlfriend in Rosenberg. The warning was to get a Texas driver's license soon and if stopped again, I'd better have one. I had lied about how long we had lived here, I told him about a month and I told him that the girlfriend was the reason we came to Texas. He let me go.

I thought about it long and hard. The risks were good that if I didn't get a real license, I would be arrested if ever pulled over again and if I did get a license, Ohio would find out where I was. I was pretty sure that states were advising each other about things like driver's licenses and warrants and arrests. I eventually decided to get a Texas driver's license and use Rhonda's address as mine, I really didn't have much choice, and I figured that if anything came of it the police would wind up going to her house first and that might buy me enough time to get us the hell out of town.

Of all the people that I came to know while at Car Craft body shop, and every one of them would help us in one way or another, one man stands out above all the others, a police officer named Rick Baker. He was a deputy constable for Precinct Five and was dating Linda. Rick was madly in love with her, although the feeling was not mutual. Linda was keeping him at arm's length while he desperately tried to win her over somehow.

Over time, Linda had told Rick about my situation and that one day I was going to need all the help that I could get. Rick would talk to me about it sometimes and eventually I became comfortable enough to tell him the whole story. He would ask if there was anything that he could do to help and at the same time he would ask me to help him get closer to Linda. Linda was a free spirit and had been around long enough to know what she wanted and how to get it. There was no telling her what was best for her and so any conversations that we had about Rick were not to his benefit. But I never stopped trying, knowing that in turn, when I needed him, he would be there. I knew that he would. He said that he knew of a very good and highly regarded lawyer and would hook me up if and when the time came. Rick was almost always in uniform when I saw him and that would have scared the hell out of me had I not known that he was on my side.

Back at school, Brian and Melissa were chugging along and doing great. I had attended every function that they were involved in and I had come to know most of their teachers and even became friends with the principal, Bertha Jamison. She is another one of the ones that I will never forget. I'll always remember how nice she was to us when she could have made it very difficult had she chosen to. Many times I was asked about school records and I was, on occasion, questioned about the mother of the kids and how the custody situation was going. I did not know it but by this time Sandy had received an uncontested divorce and full custody of the kids with my having no rights of any kind. Anyway, I always managed to talk my way out of sticky situations and had proved myself in their eyes as a very good father. We went to every carnival, every Christmas program, book sale, pillow toss, you name it. I did all of the things that a single parent does to support their children. And I didn't do it for looks, I did it because they wanted me there and I wanted to be involved in their lives as much as possible.

We played a thousand games of football in the grass at Chancellor Elementary. Most of us lived in the same complex and we would meet there on weekends to let the kids play. That was where I taught Melissa how to ride a bicycle. I still remember the way she would laugh and say, "Dad, don't let go, don't let go!" I would say, "I won't," and then I would let go every chance I could, until she was riding on her own. Once she turned to see me not holding on, she would panic and scream at me.

After the kids were asleep I would sometimes open that closet door and see the lines from when I measured them last and think about the amount of time that we had been given, figuring out how much they had grown since we left Ohio and pondering about how much time we had left. I used to ask myself how many more lines will I get to draw.

Another good memory of something that we used to do was to drive around every Christmas Eve and look at all the Christmas lights and decorations around the area and there was always a radio station in town that would break in and talk about Santa Claus sightings. The kids would hear that Santa and his sleigh had been spotted over the area and they would say, "Dad, you have to get us home quick, he's coming! We've got to get home and get to sleep so that he can come to our house." I would smile, say okay and point us towards home, all the while grinning from ear to ear.

Life was simple for us and fun was easy to find, but I was always looking at everyone around us, always trying to spot a trap, always afraid that today might be the day. Each new day brought us closer to getting caught and I knew it. Call it negative thinking, but those are the thoughts that you are faced with every day when you know that someone is looking for you. When you live that way you make the most of every minute and you appreciate every memory you collect along the way.

About this time I was approached by someone while at the church and subtly pressured to officially join the congregation. We had been stealth for a good while but people now recognized us and knew that we were regulars. Not long after that I got Father Leo off to the side and explained my story to him, telling him that the kids were not baptized per their mothers request and that I wanted to become a member and get them baptized into the Catholic faith. I told him that it was God's will that we do this. After a moment or two of pondering my story, he determined that a single father raising two children without a mother could not properly raise them in a Catholic manner and therefore he was not willing to baptize my children. I explained to him that God was in our hearts and guiding us at that very moment and that we would do just fine without him or his church. I also told him that he would never see us again and we left.

I had made as many friends as I could, I had prepared for the worst and I had never let my guard down, not for a minute. We had Rhonda taking care of us, we had mother sending us care packages whenever she could, we had moved there with what little we had in the back of a car and now we had most everything we needed.

On Wednesday, April 6th, 1983, at about 2 o'clock in the

afternoon, I got a call from Rhonda while at the body shop, she was crying and in a complete panic. She had just gotten a call at work from her oldest son, Bobby, and he had told her that a Rosenberg police officer named Mike Lorenz had just been there asking for Glen Schulz. Bobby, home sick that day, wasn't fully aware of the whole story and did what any honest child would have done; he told the policeman that we didn't live there. He told them that we lived at Brays Village apartments in Houston and that I was his mother's boyfriend. Rhonda was sobbing so uncontrollably that she could hardly get the words out and with her Southern accent, it took a while to comprehend and then even longer for it to sink in. The police knew that we were here and they knew where we lived and I needed to get my kids right now! I ran out the door of the shop telling Linda what had just happened as I raced past her. "I'll call you and let you know where we are as soon as I can," I said. I drove straight over to the school, running in the door afraid of being too late. I told Mrs. Jamison that the children's mother was here and trying to take them from me and that I needed to get the kids out of the area. They quickly helped me get the kids and we were gone. I had to think, and right now staying on the move was the safest place to be. We drove around the 610 loop in Houston, over and over again. We couldn't go home, surely they were at the apartment watching for us, waiting to arrest me and send the kids up to Ohio to their mother. Should we just leave, maybe go to Oklahoma or Florida? This time we would be leaving everything behind. Is now the time to stand and fight? Instinct told me to just go, hit I10 east and start over again somewhere. I was in panic mode. I stopped at a public phone at 610 and Telephone Road and called Rhonda, telling her that we were all right and on the move, unable to go home. She was still crying hysterically. I told her that Bobby had done nothing wrong and for her not to be mad at him in any way, this wasn't his fault or his doing at all. The inevitable had simply caught up with us. I always knew that it would one day.

Next I called Linda and told her that we were safe. I told her that I needed to talk to Rick and that I would call back in half an hour. When I called her again she gave me the number to where Rick could be reached, so I called him and we talked about what I should do next. He confirmed that there was a warrant out for my arrest and said that I should not go back home or to work for any reason until I talked to a lawyer. He gave me the name of the attorney he had mentioned before, a man named Eric Andell. He said that in the course of his work as a deputy constable he had seen Eric in court several times and that he was exceptionally good and that he had a way with people, even the judges that Rick knew thought highly of him. He gave me Eric's number and I called his office only to be told that he was not in. I told the receptionist that I needed to speak to Eric urgently and I told her why. She asked me what number I could be reached at and I explained that we were driving around with nowhere to go and that I would have to call him back. "Call back in 30 minutes," she said. We had no choice but to drive around the 610 loop at no faster than the posted speed limit and stop 30 minutes later and call him. We stopped at a Denny's to make the call. He was there and waiting for me. I told him the whole story, from start to finish. He instructed me to be at his office at nine o'clock in the morning. "Don't go home," he said, "and no motels either, they'll be scouring the area looking for you."

We must have been a sight when we arrived at his office in Greenway Plaza the next morning. We had been driving all night, I had had way too much coffee and no sleep and we hadn't had a shower or a change of clothes. Hell, we couldn't comb our hair or even brush our teeth! He introduced himself as Eric Andell and he said that he had acquired some information about us since we had spoken last evening. They were indeed looking for me on a state warrant out of Conneaut, Ohio, for kidnapping my children and the federal charge of *"unlawful flight"* to avoid prosecution. This was very serious, he said, and fighting it would be quite a feat. But he also felt that he could give me at least a fair chance to win full and permanent custody of my kids and stay out of prison. He would need a $5,000 retainer, payable immediately. A Federal charge? Holy shit, that sounded a lot worse than the state kidnapping thing sounded. I was pretty scared after hearing that part and even while listening to Eric telling me his plan, I was making my own plans. As soon as we walked out of his door we were *gone*! That five grand will go a long way towards our new lives somewhere else. That was my plan.

Mr. Andell said that he would file a petition in Harris County court that very day, April 7th, 1983. We were filing for divorce, for custody and also filing an application for a temporary restraining order stopping any and all law enforcement agencies in Harris County, Texas, from holding me in any capacity and stopping anyone from removing me or my children from the county. If granted, anyone who tried to do either of the above would be in violation of a court order. We were legal residents of Harris County he said, and we had our rights while local courts decided who had jurisdiction in the matter. If we were granted the restraining order, I could be arrested over and over, but they would not be able to hold me or remove us from Harris County unless they skirted the law to do it. He advised me to stand and fight. He said that there would never be a better time do this and that if I chose to flee again I would be pissing away any chance to ever get permanent custody. I excused the three of us so that we could go out to the car and allow myself a few minutes to make a decision.

After we closed the doors of the car it came time to either put it in drive, which was the urge that I fought with, or go back into his office and put our very future and everything that mattered to us in his hands and roll the dice. My heart told me to put the car in gear and go, but my mind told me that what he had said was true, if I leave now I will relinquish any chance to ever have legal custody of them again. I decided to put it in God's hands by way of Eric. If it is his will, it will be. I knew that God had steered me to this man, just as he had to all of the others.

I pulled the front trim panel loose in the car and pulled out my savings account and counted it out with the help of the kids. $6,380. Since I would just shove 20-dollar bills behind the panel as I could afford to, I wasn't sure just how much I had. The kids and I walked back in and I told Eric point blank that I was entrusting him to fight for our lives. I also told him that I could only give him $3,500 now, but that I would make payments on the rest each week. I fibbed a little, but I didn't intend on giving up every bit of cash that I had, just in case we needed to bail out later on. He accepted and shook my hand and we now had an attorney. He assured me that he understood my position and that he would fight for my children as if they were his own. Eric told me to go buy some clean clothes for the three of us and see if someone would put us up just long enough for him to get the paperwork in hand; someone the police wouldn't connect us with. I told him that we had a few options and that I would be back in touch. I called Linda again and she said that she would have Rick meet us at the Grandy's restaurant that evening. If anyone could make us disappear while the papers were being filed, it would be a cop. Rick met us at the restaurant, made sure we had eaten and then had me leave my car there. He had me put the car behind the restaurant and he told a supervisor inside not to have the car towed; we would be back the next day to get it. He drove us to the same motel we had stayed at when we first got to Houston, the Motel 6 at Bissonnet and Highway 59, right across the street from the body shop! In uniform he went into the motel's office while we stayed in his patrol car and when he came back he had a key to a room, damn near the same room we had lived in, just a few doors down. He said that he had told them that we were witnesses in a trial that was starting the next day and that we needed to be tucked away nameless for a few days. It was one of the most unselfish things I had ever seen, Rick risking his position in law enforcement and maybe even a felony charge of harboring us just to keep us together.

It was impossible to sleep there. I would not, could not allow the kids to open the door for any reason. No going outside, no answering the door. It was hell. I envisioned a motel employee calling the Houston Police Department and asking them why we were there and what trial we were going to testify at, in turn bringing them straight to the door and we'd be caught. I expected the police to bust the door down any minute and arrest me and send the kids to their mother. I thought for sure that our future together was gone. I thought about calling a cab to take us to our car so that we could just leave, get out before they took the kids from me. I pictured their faces as they were being dragged away from me and handed to her, all because I didn't take them and leave while we had the chance. I knelt down next to the bed that the kids were sleeping on and began to pray.

I was still on my knees five minutes later when there was a knock on the door. My heart was pounding so hard that I expected it to explode right then. The kids were asleep and I stayed absolutely silent, frozen in fear, knowing that they could gain entry by getting the office to open the door and there was no other way out. And then I heard my name. And I heard the voice. It was Rick, and he had the papers for me, copies of everything Eric Andell had filed, motions for this and motions for that. Judge John Peavey, Jr., had granted and signed a temporary restraining order barring Sandy from interfering in any way with me and the children and barring Sheriff Jack Heard from executing kidnapping warrant #265926162 or from interfering in any way with my liberty or the liberty of my children. I was also named temporary managing conservator of the minor children. My instructions were to go back to the apartment and be prepared to be arrested, maybe several times, always keeping my papers with me and trusting the system. I trusted God; I had way too much to lose to just trust the system. I called Rhonda and updated her with the news. I told her that if all went well, we would have the battle here and not in Ohio. Then Rick took us back to get our car so that we could finally go home.

When we got back to the apartment I was visibly shaking, absolutely scared to death. It was a feeling like no other, trying to trust in the system while having no trust in it at all. Trying to be somewhat in control of whatever was about to happen while knowing that I really had no control. I felt that I had relinquished my role as their father by not doing what I felt was in their best interest, disappearing again. But nothing can get you ready for your date with fate and it was here. My thoughts were that if everything went exactly as my lawyer had planned, I called it plan A, we would be okay and it would be a hell of a battle, fought right here at home. But if anything went wrong, anything at all, the children would wind up in Ohio with their mother and I would be extradited back to face the charges, never to see the kids again until I was out of prison. I wondered if they would even want to see me at all.

There was no sign that anyone had been there looking for us, no notes or papers at the door, no police camped out waiting. That queasy feeling of the unknown had set in and it was nauseating. You want to throw up, you can't eat and you have to trust the system, something that I wasn't used to. You sense imminent danger and know that you are to do nothing if it happens. We walked from room to room checking the place out as if we expected police to be under the bunk beds or hiding in a closet. Pretty soon the neighbors started showing up, concerned about us and glad to see us again. The police had been to the door of our apartment, they said, but they did not go in. They *HAD* been there, this was really happening. After all the planning, the running, the hiding, the lying, the waiting, preparing and saving, it was over, they knew where we were. They would be back. The feeling I had was as if my soul had been ripped out of my body. This meant that Sandy finally knew where we were, and it wouldn't be long before she showed up.

Two days later I put the kids back in school and I went back to work as instructed by my attorney. I simply couldn't leave things to fate so I set things up with friends that I trusted to insure that no matter what happened to me, the kids would be hidden from Sandy until there was absolutely no hope. Everyone that I trusted was on alert and ready should we need to go to plan B. And I made sure that they all knew what plan B was.

We were all standing in the front office of the body shop drinking coffee the next morning and I was updating everyone on what had been happening. The whole group was there, listening intently and very happy to see me, Linda, Jimmy, Kevin, Jeff, To and Hahn. I was telling them that there would be a hearing on April 18th to try to get the temporary restraining order turned into a temporary injunction. I could expect to be arrested, I told them, but that they would not be allowed to take me out of the county, so there was no need to panic if it happened. I thoroughly explained plan B and why we needed it just in case. Jeff Stephens was the one closest to the door and as he told me that he had a bad feeling about all this, two plain white Fords pulled in directly in front of the office door. Four men in white shirts and ties got out of the cars and two started walking toward the door. As we looked through the window, we saw more cars pull in across the street at the Mexican restaurant. We could see it all happening, it was unfolding in front of all our eyes, but comprehending it was a whole different matter. Panic set in immediately in all of us and Jeff looked at me with his face ghost white and asked me if he should lock the door. "Wouldn't do any good," I said. "They'll get in." The two men opened the door, walked in and while looking straight at me announced that they were from the FBI and were looking for Glen Schulz. "I'm Glen," I said without hesitating.

I was gently pushed up against the back wall of the office, handcuffed and searched, given my rights and brought out the door as all of my friends watched in horror. As we walked outside, I could see Sandy and Ralph standing across the street in the parking lot of the restaurant with several other men, apparently all law enforcement.

"That's him," I heard Sandy yell, "Oh my God, we got him, we finally got him." As I looked at her for the first time in almost two years, I could see the vengeful look on her face and the middle finger on her hand extended in my direction. And as my eyes crossed over to Ralph, I saw him spit towards me in some meaningless show of contempt. Everyone from inside the shop was out front now and all of them could hear the torrent of words coming from Sandy, "It's over, you bastard, I hope you like it in prison. I hope you get raped every day! You'll never see the kids again!"

I was completely overwhelmed with all of this and I thought that the worst was happening. This was the FBI, and

I assumed that they were taking me straight to the airport and to Ohio, the feds completely ignoring our little restraining orders. In a matter of minutes the kids would be scooped up and handed to her on a silver platter by a sympathetic FBI and flown back home, her ass kissed all the way and the feelings of our children disregarded entirely. I looked at my friends and co-workers with a look of fear and utter panic and yelled, "Plan B" as I was being put in the backseat of a car.

The arresting officers were very nice to me as they put me in. They asked me if the cuffs were too tight, I said no; they asked me if I wanted a smoke, I said yes; and then they gave me one and lit it. They even pulled it out of my mouth to knock the ashes off. I was very surprised. I was also shaking so bad that they didn't need to knock my ashes off for me, it was happening all by itself. Then we headed downtown to the Federal Building. They asked me what Plan B was and I told them that it was a plan I had put in place to notify our family and friends if this ever happened.

I told them that I had no hard feelings for them, they were just doing their job and they said that they indeed, had a job to do, but they hated getting involved in these kinds of actions. One of them said, "We know that sometimes the father is the best person to raise the children in a situation like this." I told them that I had papers on me that they needed to read and they said that they would look at them after we were downtown.

Plan B was being put into effect as we pulled out. Linda was calling Rick first. She was also calling Eric Andell and making him aware of what had just happened. Kevin was to call Jere' and have her go get the kids from school immediately and bring them to Jimmy, the neighbor. Jimmy was to bring the kids to a bridge we had picked out and hide with them underneath that bridge until we knew what would happen next.

Plan B was my call to make depending on whether I

thought things were going as planned or not. And when the arrest actually happened and I saw Sandy standing there with the FBI, I was afraid it wouldn't go as planned and that she would be given the kids immediately and that they would be out of Harris County before I could get out of jail, maybe even before I could talk to my attorney. If they got out of Harris County they would be beyond the range of the restraining order and forever out of our reach. The paperwork that we had filed was valid in this County only so if they got the kids into another county before we could stop them, the papers would not help. For that matter, if they could get me out of Harris County, the papers were worth nothing more than toilet paper.

The first thing that they did was to put me in a group holding cell at the Federal Building in downtown Houston. I was with several others, all of them Hispanic. I remember listening to two of them as they talked to their attorney about the drug charges brought against them, telling him "poco, poco," Spanish for a little. I heard their attorney say, "A little, my ass, you got caught with a damn truckload. Stop lying to me."

It wasn't long before I heard the voice of Eric Andell; he was telling them that they could not, not for any reason, hold me or remove me or the children from Harris County. They would be in contempt of a court order if they did. I also heard someone say that law enforcement officers from Ohio were already flying down to take me back. That iced it for me; I knew that I was a goner. It sounded like no one was listening to Eric at all. My thoughts turned to the kids. Were they okay?

Although I had no way to know it, Jere' was already under the bridge with her two children and my two. Jimmy was still at school, so Jere' had improvised and did the best thing that she could have done, get the kids to the bridge where Jimmy was supposed to take them and get them out of sight. She had no trouble at the school, she had told them what was happening and they had quickly led her and the kids to the rear exit and out the door. She told me later that our friends at the school wanted us to know that they were praying for us. In talking to Jere' about it a few days later, she said that she had been absolutely scared to death of being the one to pick up the kids. She cared for us so much, she said, that she didn't want to screw up in any way and be the weak link in Plan B. And so they huddled under the bridge, battling mosquitoes and snakes, trying to make it until word came about what to do next. When Jimmy did get there, Jere' went back to her apartment, shaking, nauseous and covered in mosquito bites. But she had not yet done all that she would do for us that day. The police were waiting and questioned her about my children when she went home.

Some time later I heard someone from the FBI saying that they had to release me per a court order. I distinctly heard him say "Can you believe that this son of a bitch has a restraining order against us?" I also remember someone saying that they had to find a way to hold me until the children could be found. That meant that they did not have them yet! They had been asking me where the children were and I kept saying that they were in Austin with some friends.

What they ultimately decided to do was instead of releasing me, they would hold me for as long as they could and then turn me over to the United States Marshals. They would then hold me as long as they could and by then, they expected that they would have Brian and Melissa. And that's exactly what they did. The restraining order stated that no law enforcement agency could hold me or put me in the Harris County jail; it did not say that they couldn't swap me from one agency to another until my attorney could stop them. Mr. Andell was doing battle with them to get me released while they were doing battle with me to get me to tell them where the kids were. I knew that it would only be a matter of time before they found the kids and the longer it took to get out of there, the better the chances the kids would be gone from me forever. They had probably been to the school already and they were probably badgering Jere' at that very moment. I didn't know how much she could endure before talking. I knew I wasn't going to tell them a damn thing.

By the time the U.S. Marshals had to release me, Jimmy had taken the kids with him and they were completely out of the area. I wish I had known that at the time, I would have felt so much better, but there was no way for me to know. They were on the opposite side of the city, sitting at Forest Park Lawndale Funeral Home, waiting for news and instructions. The only thing that I was sure of was that they hadn't found them yet because they were still asking me to cooperate. "Do the right thing for their mother," they said, "Tell us where the children are. Show us that you can put your children's best interests first and tell us."

Just about then I heard them tell Sandy that they had to let me go. I could hear her let out a blood-curdling yell of disbelief, but they told her that they had no choice. They thought about turning me over to another law enforcement agency but it would do no good, all of them would have had to hold me in the Harris County jail and we had a restraining order against them from doing that. I had been held a total of about eight hours and now they had to release me.

As they walked me out of the room and into a hallway, I saw Sandy and Ralph both standing in the doorway of an adjacent room. And when given the chance, you have to seize the moment and although I shouldn't have, I smiled, said nothing and gave them both the finger. Eric drove me to my car and then followed me home just in case there was trouble waiting for me there. There wasn't, and I immediately paid the man the remaining balance that I owed, he had already earned it in my book.

After I got home, I talked to Carol, our next door neighbor, about where her brother and the children were. He had called her and said that he would call back every so often until they had word from me or about me. When Jimmy called again, I told him I was all right and that he could come home. You could hear the sigh of relief through the phone. I had him hand the phone to the kids and one at a time, I told them that everything was okay and that I couldn't wait to give them a huge hug. Another friend had risked everything for us and could thankfully say that no mistake on their part had cost me my kids. I told Jimmy that he had done a wonderful thing for us and glowing with pride and satisfaction, he said that he was happy that he could help.

Jere' was still shaking when I found her. She began to cry while telling me about the police and how they had intimidated her when they questioned her. They had told her that she could lose custody of her own children if she didn't cooperate and help them find my kids. But she had stood firm and had told them that the children were not in Houston. She thought that they were in Austin or maybe San Antonio, she had said. I gave her a great big bear hug and apologized as I thanked her and I told her how badly I felt about all of the mosquito bites on her and her children. She had done an amazing job and I would be forever grateful for her actions.

It was then that I called my parents and told them what had happened and that I needed their help, again. After telling them that we were all right for now, I asked if they could come down and help us through this. Without a second thought, they said that they wanted to get down and be with us as soon as they could.

All of this happened so fast and so long ago, that I don't

know if I ever fully expressed my gratitude to all of these people and I would like to think that I thanked every one of them for all that they did, even more so, for all that they were risking for the three of us. Although this story was not over yet, there were so many people involved in our mess and because of my own actions, not theirs, that I still don't know how to properly thank them all. I have not forgotten any of the things that were done for us, nor the risks that were taken for us and I will certainly never forget the comfort that they provided to the three of us during all this.

Morning of temporary custody ruling 1983.

CHAPTER ELEVEN:
THE FIGHT OF OUR LIVES

I was arrested almost every day of the following week. First it was the Houston Police Department, but after they took me downtown they had to let me go because of the restraining order. Next it was the Sheriff's Department, and I had them call the Harris County jail right from the body shop to save me the trouble of finding a ride back again. Another time it was the Fugitive Warrant division of the Houston Police Department, and again I showed them my papers and they made phone calls right from the body shop while I sat there in handcuffs. First they called the Sheriff's Department and it was confirmed that they could not hold me. They actually called the Harris County jail and were told not to bring me there. Then I listened to one side of a conversation between them and the police in Conneaut, Ohio, and when the person on the other end of the phone had been told that they couldn't hold me here while they came down to get me, I could hear them raise their voice on the phone. The man on the Ohio end of the call was saying, "Don't let him go, we're on our way," and the officer here was saying "We can't hold him while you get here and you won't be able to take him out of the County anyway." And then the officer hung up and said, "Go ahead and come anyhow. I would."

The last time that I was arrested it was by the U.S. Marshals again. They took me downtown one more time and tried to turn me over to the authorities that were here from Ohio, but because of the same temporary orders, they couldn't. They called the Sheriff's Department and offered me to them, but by that time they were familiar with my name and told them not to bring me there. I was arrested and handcuffed over and over and each time I had to make sure that if anything went wrong, the kids would be safe. Plan B was still alive, waiting for me to call it into effect again if I felt the threat was there. But I knew that if they didn't get me on that first try, they weren't going to. And each time I was subsequently arrested, it was while the kids were in school, making it easy to get them if they could bend the laws.

All of the people that offered to help me right from the beginning came through for us when they needed to. With Jere' hiding the kids under a bridge and not breaking when questioned, Jimmy hiding them at the funeral home, (Jimmy was about to graduate from a mortician college and worked at that funeral home), Kevin and Christine Hayes taking the kids and hiding them at their home or with their family in New Caney, Linda hiding all three of us one time at her home, they all took risks and all went out of their way for us. With Jere' improvising when things didn't go according to plan, with Mrs. Jamison asking questions as a ruse to stall the police when they showed up at the school and then saying that the kids weren't there, because by then they weren't anymore, with Kevin's in-laws, Gilda and Mike Michaels, hiding the three of us once or twice and Rick doing the things that he did, there were just so many people involved and each with so much at risk and so much that could have gone wrong, I had no doubt that it was all happening exactly the way God wanted it to. To this day I have no doubt about God and the power of prayer.

By this time law enforcement from Ohio had flown down at least once and had been shown all of the paperwork and knew that they couldn't take me back. The Rosenberg police department was still trying to get their hands on me because they were the first to find me and they were in another County. But along with everyone else, they couldn't touch me inside Harris County. The most important thing at that point was that we didn't venture out of the county for any reason whatsoever. If we were caught outside the line, all of my papers would be invalid and they could hold us until Ohio came back down to get us, and I had no doubt that they would.

After all of the police actions came to a stop we could settle down and try to go on with life although it was still a day-to-day experience. The only difference was that we were not hiding anymore, everyone now knew exactly where we lived and our story had spread throughout the apartments. People that we barely knew were coming by to say hello or they were stopping in front of our apartment and pointing. Evidently all of the commotion was interesting to the people around us and since the story was now out about why the kids had no mother, people who had had little to do with us before were now coming by to ask questions and hear more about our story. "Tell us the whole story, please," they would say. I told many of them that one day I would write a book about it and now, over 20 years later, I finally have.

My attorney called and said that we had our first court hearing coming in a week. It didn't give me a lot of time to decide our future. Rhonda was playing a big part in our lives, my parents were making plans to be here for the hearing; we had so much support and strength to draw from coming from everyone around us that I had decided to stay and fight. Leaving now would make it a sure bet that I would never have this opportunity or this much support again. I also knew that our odds were poor at best, so it was another leap of faith. It knew it was back in God's hands again.

My parents got here and when they walked into our

apartment it felt like the weight of the world lifted off of me. It's funny how having your parents with you can do that. It was just comforting having them with us and giving us every ounce of support that they had. It assured me once again that what I was doing was right.

The first time that they met Rhonda was quite an experience for all of us. Rhonda is from a small town and she talked with about as thick a Texas accent as you can have, the epitome of a real Southern drawl. I introduced her to my parents and she chatted with them for a couple of minutes and as soon as she was out of sight, Mom and Dad both said, "What did she say? We can't understand her at all." I had to ask Rhonda to slow down and pronounce words clearly when speaking to them because they just couldn't get the "y'all" stuff. "Y'all want some ice tea? Are y'all hungry? I'm fixin' to make some dinner. Do y'all like okra?" It was hilarious and it didn't take long before they could understand her completely and by the way, they quickly grew to love the accent as much as they grew to love her.

April 18th came, the morning of our first court appearance. We were all as nervous as a cat in a house full of dogs. The hearing was in the 246th court at the Family Law Center in downtown Houston.

We all gathered in the hallway outside the courtroom and nervously paced back and forth until Eric got there. He explained that it should be a brief hearing to get things started. He was going to ask the court for a motion to extend the restraining order and it would probably be just legal wrangling, but we needed to be there just in case it went further.

Several of us were standing in a group when Sandy and Ralph stepped out of the elevator. They were with a well dressed elderly man who obviously was their attorney. He was telling them what to expect just as Eric had been doing with us.

The kids and I were there, as were my parents and a few of our closest friends. Eric had expected this to go smoothly but had them there just in case things went a different direction. It went exactly as he had planned. It was pretty much just a hearing to introduce the attorneys and begin the legal steps necessary. It was made official that Eric would be representing me and William B. Jeter would be representing Sandy. The order to extend the restraining order was granted and we were finished for the day. Another hearing was scheduled in 10 days, April 28th, that one to decide whether the children would need representation.

As tough as it was for my side, it had to be much tougher for Sandy and her side. They had to stay in a city that they knew nothing about and wait until the next hearing. We at least were at home; the temporary restraining order had done its job so far and kept us there. Ten days later we were all in court again. It was more of the legal jargon that they go through. We just sat there and watched. The restraining order was extended again and the court determined that the children needed to be represented separately rather than by Eric, so they ordered an attorney Ad Litem to be appointed for the next court date.

On May 2nd we were back in court again and attorney Joe Rentz was officially appointed Guardian, or attorney, on behalf of Brian and Melissa. We were all told to be back in court on May 5th, for something about a plea in abatement.

Eric had asked me to give him a list of people who would be willing to testify for our side and we began to write down all of the people that were volunteering. Before we knew it, we had a massive list. First and foremost was the principal of Chancellor Elementary, Bertha Jamison, who cancelled an upcoming trip overseas to be there. We also had two of the children's teachers, Mrs. Sherry Aubuchon, one of Brian's, and

Mrs. Nancy Fuller, one of Melissa's. We had the testimony of Dr. Morton Katz, Ph.D., the psychologist that had been seeing the children for some time. Then there was Doctor Phillip Bellan, our family doctor, a man that knew us well by then. They were followed by family members including my mother, father, my sister and younger brothers, Gary and Eric, both here from Boulder, Colorado. We had Rick, the police officer, Linda from the body shop, Kevin Hayes, Jeff Stephens, Jimmy Kovacs, my current boss, and Phillip Crosby, my old boss. The list also included neighbors Chuck and Lori Haynes, Jere', Carol and Jimmy Collins, Rhonda, Jeannie Hubble and others. And all of them were willing to give their time and energy to keep the three of us together. Do I need to even attempt to say how much that meant to me? Kevin even shaved his beard off for court. It was the first time his wife or any of us had ever seen him without his beard. I have a picture of him. All of these people were on standby with Eric and ready to go whenever he told them to. Until then it would just be the kids and I and my immediate family going to court each time.

May 5th came and all parties and their respective attorneys were present. It was just more legal stuff about the plea of abatement. Other than being forced to see each other over and over again it was reasonably civil with Brian and Melissa being cordial to their mother, but with obvious reservation when she was near them. I chose not to speak to her at all, as did my family, which was growing each time we went back to court. By now my oldest brother, Alan, and his wife, Jeanne, were here, as was my sister's husband, Michael. Being surrounded by family and friends during all of this was indescribable. We were fully aware that not only could something go wrong in the courtroom and the children be taken from us, but there was always the chance that given the way things were going, Sandy and her group could try to steal the kids and go back to Ohio where they would be completely legal and untouchable. We were on pins and needles not only in the courtroom, but everywhere else that we went. And we couldn't let our guard down at the apartment either, not for one second. I had already lost over 10 pounds since I was first arrested by the FBI. The possibility that I would have to give the children back to their mother was keeping my stomach turned upside down.

On May 9th we were all back in court again. Eric presented a motion to extend the temporary restraining order once again and it was granted. Sandy's attorney asked the court to arrange for visitation for her while this was going on. All parties involved agreed that it would be prudent to allow this and it was then just more wrangling while we worked out an arrangement. Under no circumstance would she be alone with them or be in a position to be able to take them out of Harris County.

Sandy would be allowed to see them in our apartment Monday through Friday from 4 p.m. until 6 p.m. On Saturdays she could see them from 9 a.m. until 2 p.m. and on Sundays from 2 p.m. until 6p.m. She was allowed to be alone with them in their room only and to have someone with them anywhere else. They could not leave the property unless Rick went with them, Rick being a deputy constable. After all of that was ironed out we agreed that I would pay $1500 and Sandy would be liable for $1000 of the retainer for Joe Rentz, the attorney for the children, with all monies to be paid prior to May 31, 1983.

On the afternoon of May 13, 1983, while I was at work, Linda came out and told me that there were two people in the office asking for me. She said that they did not appear to be police because of the way they were dressed. I followed her to the office and when I walked in, two men asked me if I was Glen Schulz. "Yes, I am," I said. I wasn't even finished speaking and they threw a bundle of papers toward me and said that they were with R.H. Wilson and Associates. It was all I could do to catch most of the papers and as I did, I asked them what it was and they responded by saying "Read it. Your game is over pal," and they walked out. It was a stack of exactly 69 pages of legal documents, mostly about a Writ of Habeas Corpus. The way I understood it, the Writ in basic form stated that there was no need for a court battle here, all issues had already been determined in Ohio and that those determinations took precedence over Texas. Eric Andell looked over the pile of papers and said that a Writ of Habeas Corpus is like a notarized birth certificate, proof of something legally documented already and normally unquestionable. He said that this would be our biggest and most difficult obstacle to overcome and virtually everything else would hinge on whether or not he could get the Writ dismissed. That was a gut check statement if I had ever heard one and for the next day or two I had second thoughts and considered pulling up stakes and heading out of town once again. We had not come this far, nor had we overcome so many things, to lose what the three of us had between us over some stupid writ. But leaving once again would leave so many friends behind, friends that really cared about us and who would then be unable to give us the help that they were offering.

The temporary orders were extended on May 18th and again on May 25th as well. The next court date would be on May 31st and it could be for all the marbles. It could be the day that the court would rule on the Writ. Life as we knew it would depend on what happened that day. Per Mr. Andell, all witnesses needed to be there for this one. We would throw everything at them and hope for the best. We had to be ready for anything.

In the meantime Sandy was coming to the apartment almost every evening. She would sit in their bedroom and play with them and read them stories. I saw it as a way for her to catch up a little on all of the things that she had missed in our absence, something that never would have happened had she not changed into a different person. It was difficult for us to bear, she was saying and doing everything that she could to win them over and gain their pity. But children have an amazing way to see through things and more often than not they couldn't wait for visitation to be over so that they could go play with their friends and be with the family.

If the worry about the Writ wasn't making me nauseous, seeing Sandy in our home groveling for pity certainly did. It got to where my parents, Rhonda, my brothers and sister and myself had to go outside and sit on the stairs out front so that we didn't get ill hearing her browbeat the kids. It was sickening.

I will never forget the day of the hearing of course; it was a matter of life and death as far as we were concerned. It was May 31, 1983. My mother took a picture of the kids and I just before we left that morning and I had been unable to sleep that prior night. The gravity of that day's event was obvious on our faces and as we walked out of the door, we took a good look around, knowing that it was very possible that we would only see it again while packing our things. I had Eric Andell, without question one of the best attorneys the city had to offer, my parents, most of my family and almost all of our friends. Sandy was there with her attorney, Mr. Jeter, a group of her friends that included Ralph, Jack and Jill and a few others. The Sheriff's Department was there, ready and waiting to arrest me, just waiting for the word to come that the Writ of Habeas Corpus would take precedence over our newly filed divorce and custody paperwork. Winning this hearing would mean a divorce and custody fight here in Houston, losing would mean handcuffs again and extradition to Ohio to face all charges, probably never to have the kids under my control again. But most of all, losing would put the kids with Sandy, something that they absolutely did not want and certainly not in their best interests at the time. I hope you can feel just a little bit of what we felt that morning, not just the kids and I, but all of our family and friends. It was a suffocating, stifling, over-whelming feeling of fear. It felt like I was wearing a corset pulled so tight that I just couldn't get enough air. I questioned my faith in God that morning as we drove downtown and I decided that losing would mean that God had abandoned us right when we needed him the most. I also knew that I had grown to trust in him and be very grateful for each and every moment and that today would be no exception. He had been with us this far.

The courtroom was completely full when Judge John Peavey, Jr., entered the room and took his seat. Eric was about to give this his all and present every witness that we had if need be; he hoped that we were ready for anything.

With little fanfare and almost inaudibly, Sandy's attorney started things off and argued that since all of this had already been decided in Ohio, why on earth would there be a question as to what to do at this point. There was nothing in question, he said, Sandy's divorce and custody were documented and in stone in Ohio and copies were presented into evidence. Mr. Jeter then began to elaborate on what Sandy had gone through for the last 21 months, unaware of the location, safety or con-dition of her children and so on. Eric objected, "Totally irrelevant to the issues at hand, your Honor," I believe that was what he said.

Eric simply said that since all of the decisions and orders referenced in the Writ were granted in Mr. Schulz's absence, he was never given an opportunity to argue or defend himself in those decisions from the great state of Ohio. Had Mr. Schulz known that a divorce and custody proceeding was taking place in Ashtabula County, Ohio, he most certainly would have argued his case at that time, rather than now while at what appears to be a tremendous disadvantage, he stated. He also made it perfectly clear that when I took the children and left Ohio, I believed that I was under no court order that restricted my parental rights to do so, neither by court order or *du jure*, and even though it was a sad fact that Mrs. Schulz was unaware of their whereabouts this whole time and she had his sympathy, Mr. Schulz believed that he had good reason to do what he did and felt that it was in the best interest of his children. Eric told the Judge that he was prepared to prove beyond any doubt that anything I had done was due to putting the children first, above all else. He then presented a Motion for Judicial Notice of Law of Ohio. It asked the Judge to consider Rule 184a of the Texas Rules of Civil Procedure in regards to Ohio Civil Rules Revised Statutes 53 A through E, and 75K. In basic terms this meant that Ohio had to prove that it mailed notices of the divorce and custody hearings to my last known address giving me at least seven days to object, and there was no evidence of that ever happening attached to the Writ.

We left the hearing for lunch and had to find somewhere to eat close by the court house. It was a time for praying, chain smoking, pacing, commode sitting, vomiting and crying. We rolled it all into one big event. And when the time came for all of us to be back in the court room, *everyone* knew that what was about to happen would affect the lives of many, although most importantly Brian and Melissa.

I haven't mentioned Eric Andell's courtroom presence, it was the first time I had seen him in hand to hand combat. I noticed early on the attention that he commanded and was given when he entered the courtroom. He had the charisma of a movie star and the sincerity of a television news anchor, albeit a humble one, and he was a man of impeccable delivery with weight to his words. I also noticed that the man representing Sandy was much older, much heavier and much more direct and to the point when speaking, almost appearing blunt. He seemed to be confused about what Eric had said and it seemed that he knew what he wanted to say; he just couldn't seem to get it out with any gravity to it. It appeared to me that he had slightly less personality and no courtroom manner per say, as if he just had a job to do and he was doing it to the best of his ability.

When Judge John Peavey, Jr., spoke you could have heard a pin drop in the room. "After hearing the pleas of both parties and after reviewing the documents presented here today in the matter of the Writ of Habeas Corpus originating in Ohio," he said, "This court finds that because the defendant is a legal resident of the State of Texas and has in fact filed for divorce and custody here in Harris County, Texas, and because the custody decision in Ohio was determined without his knowledge, thereby not allowing him opportunity to argue or object to those decisions and since said paperwork is pending in this court, I find that the decisions of the State of Ohio *do not* hold precedence here. The application for Writ of Habeas Corpus is therefore *denied*, the temporary restraining order is extended and the pending litigation will be addressed here in Harris County, Texas. This Court will convene tomorrow morning to determine temporary managing conservatorship."

Wow. Holy shit! "Thank you, Lord" was all I could say as the tears flowed without restraint. What a relief! We would get to stay here and stay together for now. All three of us could go home! The emotions ran rampant in all of us and unfortunately, in view of Sandy and her group. We had just overcome a major hurdle; yet we knew that we had a huge fight looming in the weeks ahead. But at that particular moment it was time to celebrate and time to eat a good meal. On the way home almost 30 of us stopped at a Black Eyed Pea Restaurant and celebrated the decision with a victory party. Many of us had gone several days unable to keep much food down and it was time to pig out. Of course my father insisted on paying the bill.

The following morning we were all back in court again, Sandy and her group of supporters and the children and I with our circle of support. The three lawyers took turns speaking about what they felt was in the best interest of the children and with two out of the three in agreement, the Judge granted me temporary managing conservatorship during the interim and a new court date was set. It would be the start of the biggest battle, the one that determined permanent custody and it would begin on June 13, 1983.

Now it was time to prepare for the big fight. We went over all of the possible witnesses in our behalf and how many would be able to testify for us, sort of our own voir dire. It was a pretty strenuous ordeal. We had to try to weed out the ones that could easily get confused and the ones with a problem in their past that could make their testimony less credible. It still came down to an impressive list. My attorney felt that we had a strong chance to succeed if we presented our case properly and that would include testimony from family, friends in Houston that knew us as the single parent family that we were and as many professional witnesses as we could muster. The list held my parents, brothers Alan, Gary and Eric, my sister Linda, Rhonda, Jimmy and his sister Carol, Jere', Buford, Kevin, Jeffrey Stephens and his girlfriend Carol, Chuck and Lori Haynes, Jeff Glaser and others. It also had Jimmy Kovacs, Linda Yokem, Rick, the deputy constable, Mrs. Bertha Jamison, the principal of the school who had cancelled her trip to be there, Mrs. Sherry Aubuchon, one of the teachers at the school and Doctors Phillip Bellan and Morton Katz. To this day I cannot express my appreciation enough for the selfless acts of kindness shown at that time. In total we had at least 27 people ready and willing to testify for our side.

On the morning of June 13th, we were as scared as you can get. There was always the possibility that things could change and begin to go in Sandy's favor. Perhaps proof might surface that those letters from the court in Ohio were actually sent to my last known address. Maybe the Judge would have a sympathetic moment and award Sandy temporary custody while she was here fighting for her children, only for her to disappear like I did. Lots of thoughts went through my mind, enough to drive Eric nuts with my never ending questions and fears. But that was me, worry about everything and even then feel like you didn't cover all of your bases. Living on the run had taught me to be that way; it was now instinct.

I was with my parents and friends waiting for court to begin and several of us had decided to go outside and smoke. We were standing in front of the elevator doors awaiting our turn when the door opened and it was Sandy and her group of witnesses. In the group were some of my friends from years gone by up in Ohio, some of my in- laws on Sandy's side, and Ralph, Jack and Jill. When the door opened and we all saw each other, it was quite a shock to both sides, my whole group just inches away from her whole group at that moment.. The tension was thick enough to cut. My father said later that he almost had a heart attack over it.

The morning started off with us allowing the kids to spend a little time with their mother in the hallway and in an adjoining room prior to the start of the hearing. Eric felt that it would be a nice gesture and it would maybe go a long way in helping us out in the days to come. They would not be testifying, so there was no fear of Sandy intimidating them beforehand.

When court began, there seemed to be a lot of jostling

around going on up at the front of the courtroom. Each lawyer seemed to be getting set for their respective chance to do battle, trying to pick the right chair position and plan their moves out. It was probably 10 a.m. when Eric Andell said witnesses would begin testifying. I had the majority of my witnesses there, with most of the professional ones simply awaiting a phone call and they would be there. A rule was put in place right off the bat where those who were going to testify would not be able to hear those who were testifying, so when the first witness was called, all others witnesses were ordered out of the courtroom. Everyone there to testify for either side was confined in the same small hallway outside the courtroom and the emotions were running very strong. My entire family was ushered out there, and they were extremely disappointed that they wouldn't get to hear all of the lies and the bullshit that would soon spew forth from Sandy's side. And there was nowhere for you to go so you just sat or walked up and down the hall, everyone intermixed together and in almost complete silence.

Eric Andell had decided that I would not testify. He felt that I would get too emotional when questioned by Sandy's attorney and that I'd say things that might not be in our best interest. Because of that decision I would be able to stay in the room and watch the whole thing unfold. The first thing that happened was the playing of a recorded deposition from Dr. Morton Katz, Ph.D. He was unable to attend and so Joe Rentz, the children's attorney, had deposed him prior to the trial. It was made clear by Dr. Katz that taking the children from their father would be a crucial mistake. He testified that the children were in good mental health and disrupting their lives could only have a negative impact on them. Mr. Jeter could offer no resistance to this because he had paid an independent psychologist of their choosing to talk with the children and his results were not in Sandy's best interests and therefore not presented in court at all.

It was now time for the first live witness to be called, and it would be Sandy. I have no idea why she was put on the stand first, I think that it was a decision made by either her attorney, Mr. Jeter, or the childrens attorney, Joe Rentz, I'm not sure, but I know that Eric was very surprised.

Her attorney ran her through the sequence of events that led to my taking the children and between them they made it sound like I was a cold-blooded, child molesting, worthless enema bottle. Her answer to every question was that I needed to pay for what I had done to her. I needed to go to prison, I needed to pay two years of back child support to her, I needed to pay her legal fees and expenses now and in Ohio—oh, and one more thing, I needed to rot in hell. Fine. I understood how she felt, I really did. I didn't quite agree, but I did understand. It was exactly how I knew that she would feel. I had thought about it many times in the silence late at night. After two years, I still knew her pretty well.

We broke for a break and I went out into the hallway to see the kids and the family and friends and everyone was asking me what was happening inside. I couldn't tell them of course, they were witnesses waiting for their turn. All I could tell them was that Sandy was on the stand and soon to be questioned by Eric Andell.

Back in the courtroom and with almost no provocation from Eric, Sandy quickly began to lash out at me and come undone. She was upset and she began cussing about me and about what I had done to her. "Two years," she said, "Two years without knowing where they were. Two years of child support and alimony that needs to be repaid." She said that I had unpaid bills up north that I had been ordered to pay in the Ohio divorce decree, and that I needed to pay them or she would have to. She said that she was going to lose her job because of the fact that she was tied up down here and her husband, at her side all the time, was losing income as well. Eric asked her about all of the times that the children were with babysitters while in her care. He asked her if she felt that the way of life she had been giving them was in their best interests or in her best interests. He asked her about the restraining order accusing me of sexually abusing the children. He got her to admit that the charges were false, simply an easy way to separate me from the children because she was pissed. The vindictiveness was ever-present, as was the spitefulness. She was showing her true colors in an unsympathetic manner, winning over no one in the room.

With Sandy crying, the court recessed for lunch and we all went out into the hallway where all of our friends were patiently waiting. They wanted desperately to hear about what was happening, but neither side could say a word other than that Sandy was still on the stand. We walked down the street and found somewhere to eat, or at least try to. I wanted so badly to tell them about what was happening inside, although they never asked. They were concerned and they cared, but they knew I couldn't tell them. All I could tell them was that Sandy was still being questioned.

When court resumed Sandy was called back to the stand and was as belligerent as ever, bothered very much by the fact that she was the one being interrogated instead of me. She was furious about it and attempted to ask Judge Peavey why she was being grilled when I was the one in trouble. But she was stopped in her tracks. A witness can't sit there and ask the judge a question like that. Eric got her ever so close to the brink of losing it completely, so much so that she could not keep calm during the questioning. Eric had hit home when he asked her why she had moved out of our home and had the phone disconnected the day after we allegedly went missing. She had no logical explanation and it was disastrous for her. And if she expected things to get better when Joe Rentz took his turn, she was mistaken. Joe had only one, well actually two, things on his mind: Brian and Melissa. He wanted to know just how the kids had been fitting into her life prior to my taking them. "What had been your priorities back then and what are they now?" "My children", was her reply. "Mrs. Schulz, should we depose your old neighbors, Dave and Berdell Seibert?" he asked.

When Sandy had finished testifying, Judge Peavey called for a meeting in his chambers with the children, along with the three attorneys. I can still see my children's faces as they were being led away, looking back at me as if asking for my assurance that they would be okay going with the lawyers. The rest of us sat in the courtroom or outside in the hallway and waited. And then suddenly they came out of the chambers and when Judge Peavey walked in, court was again called into session.

Judge Peavey began to speak and he said something very much like this, "In the case of Schulz vs. Schulz, this court has listened to the mother of the children speak for several hours. And in those hours this court has never once heard her say that she missed her children. This court has never once heard her say that she loved her children or that nothing else mattered more than their well being and happiness. In fact, all that was mentioned was her bitterness towards Mr. Schulz. We have also spoken with the children in chambers and we have reached a decision which we believe to be in their best interests. It is hereby ordered and decreed that Mr. Schulz is appointed managing conservator of the minor children and that Mrs. Schulz shall have supervised visitation rights." The judge then said that "Mrs. Schulz will be permanently enjoined from pursuing any further legal action and ordered to take all action necessary to dismiss any criminal actions against Mr. Schulz originating in Ohio." And court was dismissed.

The kids and I were awarded the opportunity to go out into the hallway and tell everyone out there, our side, her side and anyone else in range, that this battle was over and their testimony would *not* be needed at all. "It's over," I said. "We won!" I was crying, stunned by what had just happened and virtually unable to speak. Eric had to explain it for me. No one, including my attorney had expected things to happen the way that they did. Everyone was shocked and in disbelief. It was over. I would *not* have to give the children back, I would *not* have to go to prison and there would be no more hiding or running ever again. It was a stunning and completely unexpected conclusion and after the initial shock wore off, we lined up to thank Eric and Joe for the no less than stellar job that they had done. My family and friends could only go by the information that I could now relay to them, but they too, couldn't find the appropriate words to say in gratitude. I never got the opportunity to thank the judge. I'd like to meet him one day and buy him a cup of coffee. I'd like him to know just how thankful we are to this day. I want him to see for himself how well the children turned out and I want him to know that it is in part because of him. Yes, I raised them, but it was only because of God and him that I got the chance. I believe to this day that had it been any other judge, I might have been separated from my children, perhaps with no contact with them from that point on. God bless you John Peavey, Jr.

Melissa and Brian 1984

CHAPTER TWELVE:
A SURPRISE ATTACK

It was the summer of 1983 and for the first time since we left Ohio, I didn't have to worry about being found. The problem was that all of the rulings were only for Harris County. Anywhere else in the country and the Ohio ruling held precedence. If I was found by the police outside of the county, or if we were being watched by Sandy or someone hired by Sandy and they could call the police if they saw us leave the county, we would be bound for Ohio because of the outstanding warrants still valid. And so when we were deciding to go to a movie, or Astroworld or anywhere else, I always made sure it was within the county.

At Car Craft, Linda had it out with management and decided to go open her own body shop and almost all of us went with her. She opened Linda's Extraordinary Paint and Body. Kevin, Jeff and I all went with her while To and Hahn stayed at Car Craft and became the head body man and painter. Linda had a lot of friends in the business and as soon as we opened, the work just came. Rick was still trying to have a permanent relationship with her and as always, he was relentless in asking for my help. I felt that I owed him for all that he had done for us, but I could never repay him in the manner that he wanted most, Linda's love. He had ours, he had the love of my parents and all of my family, but he never really had hers.

I was still seeing Rhonda, but because she lived outside of the county I couldn't go see her and that made it hard on her.

She had such a big heart and so much on her plate, a single mother with two boys and working a full-time job, taking care of her mother and coming to see us whenever she could. Looking back, I wish I had done more to make life easier for her. I believe that she loved my children more than their own mother ever did. I know that she loved me.

Later that summer, I took Brian and Melissa to Astroworld and its sister park Waterworld one day and we rode on every ride that they wanted to ride and as many times as they wanted to ride it. It had been a tough year and they had earned all of the fun that they could have. The kids saw that Billy Idol was going to be there in concert that night and they wanted to see him and I said okay. We went into the amphitheater early and stood in front of the stage wanting to be up front so that the kids could see him. It was extremely hot that evening and we were sweating while we stood there waiting for the concert to begin. People started gathering around us and before we knew it we were being pushed further and further back by the crowd. With two kids with you, it's hard to stand your ground in a sea of hot, rowdy, sweaty, beer-drinking people and all we could do was go with the flow. Just before the show started, park employees began to throw ice into the crowd from the stage to try to cool things off a bit. Then they started squirting water into the crowd, completely soaking people at random and it was becoming unbearable for us. By the time the concert started and Billy Idol took the stage, we had been pushed so far back that the only way for the kids to see the stage was if I put them on my shoulders, which I did, one at a time. And by the time he sang "White Wedding," the smell of pot was so bad that Brian vomited all over and Missy was turning a funny color herself. It turned out to be a big disappointment for all of us and I got us out of there immediately.

Raising children is fun and funny things happen, things

that you never forget. One of those things still makes me smile each time I think about it. I got home from work one evening and Brian told me about an ad for a movie that he had seen on television that afternoon. I told him that we could go see it that weekend and then I asked him where it was playing. He said "at a theatre near you. Dad, do you know where that one is?" I asked him which one, and he said "that theatre near you. Do you know where it's at?" It was just like an old Abbott and Costello skit and just made me laugh over and over again.

One day I saw a commercial on television that said Continental Airlines had just started a shuttle flight from Hobby Airport on the south side of Houston to Intercontinental Airport (now George Bush) on the north side. For 25 bucks you could fly from one airport to the other. Knowing that the kids had never flown before, one Saturday I drove them to Hobby Airport and bought three round-trip tickets to Intercontinental Airport and back. The lady at the ticket counter thought I was nuts. She said that she had never sold round-trip tickets from Houston to Houston before and looked at me like I was not playing with a full deck. When times like that happen, I don't try to explain, I just don't give a shit what they think. We boarded the plane and a stewardess asked the kids where they were flying to and they said nowhere and looked at me smiling. The stewardess was obviously confused so I spoke up and explained that it was their first taste of flying and that this was the perfect flight to break them in with. She agreed with me and pinned wings on both of the kids in honor of their first flight and announced to all on board that we were flying round-trip from Houston to Houston. We deplaned at Intercontinental, had something to eat and walked around the airport and then boarded again when we were ready for our return flight to Hobby. They loved it. It was a perfect way to spend the day and let them experience flying.

The rest of 1983 went by in a blur and things began to settle down into a reasonably normal life for us. That Christmas
I could afford to buy them both bicycles. Riding bikes on the
sidewalks of the apartment complex was against the rules,
although there was never a day that you didn't see someone
doing it. Shortly after Brian got his bike, the security man at
the apartment complex, an older man named Bill Keeler, took
the bike from him and locked it in the offices for two weeks.
As soon as Brian got his bike back, Mr. Keeler took it away
again. This time I contested to no avail and realized that Mr.
Keeler simply did not like my children. I think it had to do
with his beliefs, like maybe kids should be raised by their
mother and mine were not. Or it may have been related to our
notoriety within the complex. Anyway, I learned enough about
the man to know that he could kiss my ass. The following
summer he took Brian's bike away for two months. Two
months! For doing what almost every other kid was doing, riding it on any part of the sidewalk. He made it very clear that
he didn't like either of the kids and later on when we needed
him the most, he would be no help at all.

Brian was playing football in the Alief youth league and
trying to get him to each practice and also be at every game
was a little tough. One time I was late getting to one of his
games at Fun Stadium and had to bring Melissa in her paja-
mas. I had told her to be ready and she had dragged her feet
about it so I made her go just as she was. She was always ready
after that.

The whole apartment complex seemed to know about us
now. We held a sort of celebrity status in the immediate area
and more and more people would say hello or come by just to
talk to me. I was almost always at my usual perch, sitting on
the steps in front of the apartment, always watching for signs
of trouble and always available to chat with anyone who

wanted to have a cup of coffee with me and talk. And every-one that knew me knew that I always had coffee ready.

In 1984 my divorce became final in Harris County, Texas. and I was officially a single man again, but only in this county. My divorce and custody meant nothing anywhere else because there was still an active arrest warrant out for me everywhere else in the country. But in the county, I was a divorced single parent with custody of my two kids. Sandy was given visitation rights and was also ordered to pay child support, something that she never did. In fact, in order for her to have the children, she had to contact me first and then come to Houston and since she never paid any support, I never allowed her to have the kids. I know, you're thinking that I was an asshole, but really, if she had taken the kids out of Harris County, I would've never seen them again. I wasn't trying to keep the kids from their mother; I was just trying to keep the kids.

Life was not only good, it was very good. And we were very grateful. We had plenty of friends checking on us all the time, and Rhonda and her boys came over once or twice week. I was the kind that could be a mother when I needed to be and a father the rest of the time. Rhonda was having a much more difficult time of it trying to be a father when she needed to be. I tried to be a father to her boys when I could, but we didn't see them often enough. We couldn't go there and when she came to see us it was usually when the boys were with their father for his visitation.

I had learned how to cook pretty well and always liked to bake so I was usually baking something every weekend, some-times cookies, other times cupcakes or brownies or a bundt cake. I have pictures of Eric from upstairs sneaking down to eat them whenever he could.

By late 1984 we had pretty much put all of our problems behind us and we had settled into a life of freedom and happiness, albeit limited to Harris County. And then out of nowhere one Saturday afternoon as I was baking cookies and watching the kids play out front with several other children, I stopped watching long enough to take the cookies out of the oven. As I did I heard Jeremy, one of Brian's best friends, yelling through the open door, "Missy's mom's got her in a car." I stopped what I was doing and said "What?" "Missy's mom has got her in a car!" he said again. "Where?" I yelled. "In back of the apartments," he said. I did not hesitate, this was something that we had talked about over a hundred times, something we had planned for, but when something you plan for never happens, you begin to let your guard down and I had. Briefly, in fact just a few seconds, but I had. I ran out of the door and as I passed Carol and Jimmy's apartment to our left, I yelled that Sandy was here and trying to steal the kids. I screamed that I needed Jimmy's help and that I needed Carol to call the police. When I got to the parking lot at the back of the complex, I saw a car parked parallel with the fence and with the passenger door open and I could hear my daughter screaming from inside of it. I ran to the open door and Missy started reaching for me from the middle of the back seat as soon as she saw me. I was reaching for her, too, and as our hands touched someone pulled me backwards from behind. It was Tim Andrews, an old friend of ours from Ohio. He was pulling me backwards in a bear hug and I was swinging wildly, hitting him as many times as I could from the position that I had. Tim started yelling at his wife, Leslie, another close friend of Sandy's that I hadn't had time to notice but was sitting behind the wheel. "Get out of here. GO! Get going NOW! I'll find my own way back to Ohio." He was screaming at the top of his lungs and he was now between me and the open car door. My daughter was in the backseat being held by her mother and someone else, screaming as loud as she could, calling out "Daddy, Daddy," as she fought to get free.

She had wet her pants in sheer terror while scratching and clawing at her mother to free herself. Just as Leslie put the car in gear and floored it, Jimmy Collins came up behind Tim and grabbed him around the neck, pulling him off of me and allowing me time to try to reach into the now-moving car. The passenger side door swung shut and the top of it hit me square in the forehead as I leaned in to make a grab for the steering wheel and looked ahead trying to find something to steer towards. Blood was now running down my face and dripping onto my shirt. I reached for the wheel as the car was going forward and fended off the barrage of arms trying to push me away. I grabbed it and pulling hard to the right, forcing her to hit two cars in the parking lot and come to an abrupt stop.

By the time the car stopped, the blood was staining my t-shirt and Missy was beyond panic-stricken. I pushed Sandy away, grabbed and pulled my daughter with all my might and extracted her from the backseat before anyone could stop me, while Sandy was biting my arms and Leslie was trying to stab me with a nail file. Tim and Jimmy were fighting it out about 30 feet away and I stood there for just a moment with my daughter tightly in my arms, blood dripping, wondering what to do next. I wanted to go help Jimmy, but couldn't put my daughter down and wouldn't risk putting her in a position where she could be hurt either.

As I gathered my thoughts and my senses, I realized that my son was nowhere to be found. And in a second or two, the Houston Police pulled in, two cars showing up simultaneously. The officers ran towards the car and after the many witnesses now gathered around us pointed to Sandy and her friends as being the bad guys, they were all handcuffed. While that was happening I began to search for my son, not knowing if he had already been taken in a different car and was on his way out of the county or not. If so, what is he thinking and feeling? Is he okay? How do I get him back? I was stricken with fear. And I started running and calling his name.

Running through the apartments and carrying my daughter and yelling for my son all at the same time, I heard him call out "**DAD!**" And then I saw him coming out from behind a Pepsi machine next to the door of the apartment's laundromat. He said that when he saw his mother and some strangers putting his sister in a car, all he had time to do was hide behind the closest thing that he could find and stay there. "Good boy," I said as I held him and his sister both, not about to let go for any reason.

After the police had time to look at Sandy's legal papers which showed that she had full custody and after they had called in and found that there was a warrant out for my arrest, they took the handcuffs off of Sandy and the others and put them on me. They were going to give the kids to their mother and take me to jail! I desperately tried to tell them that I had my own papers from right here in Harris County, but they were determined to arrest me and give my kids away. I had Jimmy and Jere' go to our apartment and get my papers from on top of the kitchen counter and I had Carol call Rick and tell him to get there ASAP, and then I pleaded with the police to *not* give the kids to Sandy until Rick could get there. I explained that they would be in violation of a court order if they let the kids leave with their mother, not knowing if that were even true any longer or not.

As they were talking to someone on the police radio, Rick came flying in from the far end of the parking lot, his white car with Constable on the sides coming to a stop sideways about a hundred feet from the Houston Police cars. Wearing just a t-shirt and shorts, he jumped out quickly and showed them his badge. He had been in the process of getting his hair cut by Linda, no less, when he got the call at her house. Carol had gotten no answer at Rick's and had then called Linda. As he got out and flashed his constable badge at the police officers and identified himself, his handgun fell from his waistband and bounced on the pavement. "Rick Baker, Precinct Five, I'm taking control of this situation," he said. I don't really know why, but the Houston Police officers put up no fight that I can remember and Rick undid my handcuffs and gave them back to the officers, who were looking over my papers at the time. The children were sitting in a police car with Sandy at that very moment and she was sure that I was going to jail and that she was going to Ohio with both of our kids. But Rick took the kids out of the police car, handed them to me and listened while Sandy gave him a dose of pure hell. As the Houston Police were writing reports about the damaged cars, Rick was putting cuffs back on Sandy and making her sit on the grass near the wrecked cars. He told her to watch her mouth more than once and threatened to cuff all her friends if she didn't calm down. I'll bet that she was madder than she had ever been in her entire life. I knew that it wasn't a good time to tell her that this was God's will, but I wanted to. And I knew that it was. *Dominus Vobiscum.*

We had attracted quite a crowd. There were probably more than 80 people standing there watching all of this unfold. And one of them was Mr. Keeler, the beloved security man at the apartments. I realized that he had never once gotten involved and I couldn't understand why.

Rick had saved us again. He felt that the best thing to do at that point was to let Sandy cool off and let the children settle down. We sat out there while he did paperwork on the whole thing and by then Linda came. She was about halfway done with cutting his hair when he had jumped up and ran to help us. Rick and Linda *had been together* at the time of the emergency call, maybe there was hope for them after all. Rick decided that it would be best if we all went to our apartment to have coffee and talk about the situation.

You can probably imagine how we all felt, Sandy knowing just how close she had come to getting the kids and getting away, me and the kids having her in our home again, our little comfort zone, the place that she had so desperately wanted to find those first two years. But now she was there, in our home and drinking coffee, and it was strange indeed. I can't say that we parted friends or with any agreement between us, in fact, we barely spoke. I wasn't as mad at her as I was at myself for letting my guard down, if only for that one minute and for my not being as prepared as I had always been. In the end, Rick escorted them out of Harris County and told them that if they ever tried this again, he would arrest them and they would sit in jail in Houston.

After Sandy was gone and we could talk about what had happened, I found out that as her group was trying to catch Missy, they had cornered her and scared the heck out of her. She had run to Mr. Keeler, who happened to be in back, and she had wrapped herself around one of his legs in a panic and explained that her mother was trying to get her. Mr. Keeler had supposedly said something to the effect that this was not his kind of problem and he pushed her away and chose to just watch things unfold. It became obvious how he felt about us and that is why Jimmy had to pull Tim off of me while Mr. Keeler just watched.

The kids and I were at Kroger's grocery shopping one day and as we walked up to the checkout area the kids pointed to a woman working at one of the registers. "That's Heather's mother," they said. "They live in our apartments." I looked at her and recognized her from the apartments and we got in her line. She was very nice to us and said that she knew who we were. She said that her name was Debbie and, yes, she was

Heather's mother. The kids knew who Heather was, I did not. I thanked her, told her that it was very nice to meet her and we left without another thought about it.

We had some friends in the apartments named Jenny and Harry Peterson and they had a daughter named Holly. Jenny had approached our door first, her being the boldly curious kind. She stopped by sometimes as she passed our door and asked blunt questions with no guilt or shame whatsoever. Obviously, she just had to know why Sandy and I had split up and why all this commotion was going on. I tried to downplay everything as I normally did, but over time she would come back and pick and pick, slowly but relentlessly, until she got the answers she wanted. Jenny kept asking me if she could hook me up with a friend of hers, someone she worked with and I continually told her no thank you, Rhonda and I were together and just fine, thank you anyway.

After a while all the drama died down and we settled back into our lives once again. The kids were doing just fine in school and were involved in all the things that kids get involved in. The kids enjoyed sports, hobbies, school plays, Christmas vespers, friends at the apartment and sometimes even sleepovers somewhere else. We were still missing all of the family reunions and get-togethers at the holidays back home, but it was a small price to pay to have the life that we had. And we were all right with that. We always knew that we could not leave the county, not for any reason. Although I had legal custody, it was still only valid here. Anywhere else, especially home, and I would be in deep shit. Spend just one week making sure that you don't cross outside of the county lines that you live in; it's harder than you think.

Things started to go bad at work after a while. Linda was great to work for; it was just that being around her all the time kept me uneasy with Rick, where my true indebtedness and loyalty grew to be. Although Linda had been more than a friend, even letting us hide at her home one time when we needed to, Rick had become our superhero, or superman rather, and I felt that I owed him more than I could ever repay. And the only thing that I could do for him, other than painting his car when it needed it, was to keep trying to get him and Linda permanently together. Try talking a woman that you have always wanted to sleep with, into loving someone because you owe that person. And seeing Linda on a daily basis and knowing that there was more to Linda's life than Rick put me in a bad spot. Not to mention that everyone around her wanted to sleep with her, including those wrecker drivers, bankers and most of the vendors that came in the door. Anyway, it wasn't long before I realized that I could not get her to fall in love with Rick and he was never going to stop asking me to help. "Did you tell her this? Did you say that? What did she say? Do you think she really meant it?" Finally I got into a position where I knew Linda was spending the weekend with someone and Rick badgered me about where she was and I finally told him. I didn't do it to hurt anyone, it just came out. It was the truth and I felt that he deserved the truth. How the hell do you lie to one of the people that helped you keep your children? It spelled the end for me at Linda's, I could not stay and be confronted by her about why I told him, and so I had no choice but to pack my tools and leave. And I did it while she was gone. Jobs were easy to find in a city as big as Houston anyway, they always were. Later I went in and explained to her what I had done and why, and although she was mad at me, she hugged me and wished me and the kids good luck. "You don't have to leave, you know," was the last thing she said.

"Thanks, but yes, I do," I answered.

I went to work for Mossy Oldsmobile soon after that and I could again focus on making money instead of all of the relationships that I had formed. It felt good. I buckled down and made some money in a place where no one knew about my life. The past was the past and it could now stay there.

I was at work one day and they paged me to the office for a phone call, something I rarely got at work. It was the school asking me how much longer Brian would be out sick. I told them that he was not sick and that I would get to the bottom of this. I did what I knew would get a response, I called home. I knew my son and I knew that if I called and let it ring and ring and ring, forever if necessary, it would drive him nuts and sooner or later he would answer it. Brian didn't have a lot of patience in that way. I knew that he would get fed up and eventually answer the phone if he was there. "What do you want?" is how he answered in a mad and impatient tone of voice. "What do you think you are doing?" was my response. "You're butt is in big trouble mister," I told him, "Do not leave the apartment for any reason. And do not open the door for anyone."

Brian was beginning to show the signs of a troubled child; I just didn't recognize them. All of the running, the hiding, the seeing his mother in the courtroom, showing her his prized comic book collection in his room while being put on some guilt trip and then saying goodbye again only to hide behind a soda machine later, all of it was getting to him and I never saw it coming. He had not turned in his homework and had not done it, so he just figured that he would just never go back.

Jenny called me late one evening, maybe about 11 p.m. and said that Debbie had rented a house just down the street from the apartment complex on Bandlon and that Debbie had just called her saying that someone was trying to break into her house. Jenny and Harry had moved into a home about a mile away and couldn't get there as fast as I could. I barely knew who Debbie was, but I knew that she was a single parent with a daughter and that she needed help right now. Jenny said that she had called the police and they would be on the way, but getting there now might mean saving someone's life. I locked the door to the apartment, the kids sound asleep and I ran across the parking lot to see if I could help. By the time I got there the police were already there, so I just walked past rather than disrupt them, I didn't know these people anyway and I didn't want to be anywhere near a bunch of police officers. After I walked past and had turned around to go home, a police officer stopped me and started grilling me about what I was doing there. I had to ask for Debbie so that she could tell them that I wasn't the bad guy; I was only there to help. Debbie was grateful that I made the effort that night and we began a friendship. I had lived in fear for years, but not the kind of fear a single mother must go through when they live without a man to protect them.

About July of 1985, I realized that with the kids growing up and with all the stuff that we were accumulating, we needed more room. And so I rented a house on Holworth Drive, almost right across from the apartments. It was a house of our own, with bedrooms upstairs and a large living room with a fireplace. I bought a used living room set from a family moving out of state and we simply carried everything we owned across the street. We left our yellow naughahyde couch in the apartment, hopefully to help the next renters. We loved having our own home and the kids had their own rooms for the first time in their lives.

Rhonda was still coming over every other weekend and now I was working at Frank Gillman Pontiac. We body men always think that the grass is greener somewhere else, but it never really is. The word had spread through Mossy that Gilman was paying more per hour, so a few of us left. Some people stay where they are, due either to loyalty or comfort I suppose, I'll go to where they pay the most. Loyalty doesn't pay bills and they don't accept it at the store. I believe that we are a commodity while we are worth something to someone and the day will come when we are not, so get what you can while you are worth something. I had come to make a good friend while I was at Mossy Olds, a fellow Yankee named Jeb Vise. Jeb and I got along great and the kids and I started going over to his house occasionally. Jeb's wife Grace took to mothering us as if we were her family. Jeb and his family were meeting us about once a week for supper too, usually at the Pizza Inn on Bellaire. Tuesdays were the all-you-could-eat buffet nights, so we would meet there and enjoy each other's company. Jeb was from Long Island and had quite an accent, almost as hard to understand as Rhonda's. They had a daughter about the same age as my daughter, Lisa, and two older boys already on their own.

I began making new friends at Gillman, one of them being Joe Serrano, another body man working there. Joe was a little older than me and would show me how to take things apart on cars that I had never worked on before. On each new model car they hide the bolts and screws and you have to hunt for them, and hunting takes time and time is money. A common courtesy as a body man is to enlighten others about things like that when you have the chance. Joe's wife's name was Pety and they lived near us and had three sons all around the ages of my children. I introduced Jeb and Grace to Joe and Pety and before long we were all meeting at the Pizza Inn on Tuesday nights. Jeb quit Mossy and came to work with us at Gillman. At times when my parents or other family members were down to see us, we would all meet at the Pizza Inn and pig out. We would put a serious dent in their all-you-can-eat buffet every time we went.

I was at work one day in early 1986 when Brian called me and said that his mother was outside the front door of our house. He had walked over to the house from across the street at the apartments where he was supposed to be. Jere' was still meeting the kids at the school and watching them until I got home over at the apartments and Brian had walked over to the house to get something. He was 12 at the time and old enough to understand things knew how to follow the rules. As he unlocked the front door, his mother started calling him from a car parked just down the street. Brian recognized her and panicked, quickly running inside and locking the door. When he called me, he said that he was standing inside the front door holding his BB gun, ready to use it if necessary and his mother was outside the door trying to coax him into opening the door. I got off the phone and told Joe that I had a crisis at the house and had to go now, and he said that he was going with me in case I needed help, and after remembering how badly I needed help the last time, I agreed. On the way there I explained to him that Sandy was attempting to steal them again.

When we got there, Sandy and some of her friends were parked on the street and they immediately took off when they saw me pull into the driveway. I didn't know if they had Brian with them or not or for that matter Melissa, either, so I had to open our door and find out before giving chase. Brian was safely inside, smiling as he told us about how he was ready to shoot if necessary, but he said that he didn't know if they had Melissa or not. I threw the door open, leaving Joe to stay with my son and ran over to the apartments, praying on the way that she had not been taken.

She was with Jere' and was safe. After we walked home, I squeezed them both tightly and thanked God again. For about the millionth time now, he had taken care of us. We drove around for a while trying to find them, wondering if they would be back tonight, tomorrow or another day. I tightened all reins on the kids again. This was the second time she had tried to steal them and I knew that she might never stop. I knew that I would never stop if it were me.

Years later we found out that Sandy was so disheartened by that last episode that she had decided to never try again. Knowing that Brian had the chance to hop in the car willingly and leave with her but chose not to, she figured that they really did want to stay with me. I believe that until that day she honestly thought that the children wanted to be with her up north and that she thought that I was holding them against their will. She told Brian and Melissa years later that coming to the realization that they really had not wanted to be with her had been a devastating blow.

The kids were growing like weeds and we were still doing all of the things families do: football, school events, movies, good times and bad times. The kids were now 13and 11, respectively, and I was trying my best to keep them seven and six again, just like when we left.

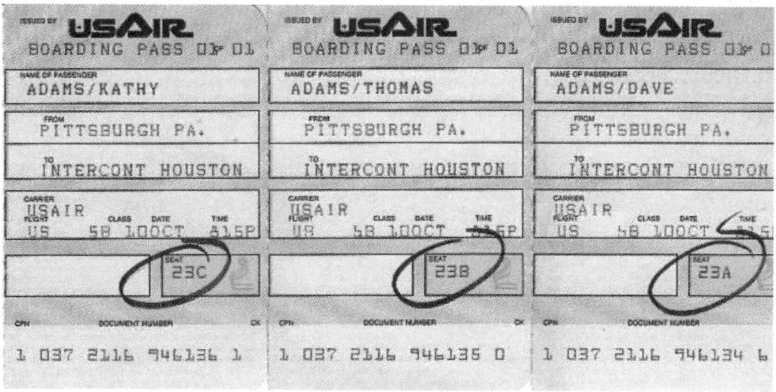

Escaping under false names in 1988.

CHAPTER THIRTEEN:
NO DONUTS HERE

It was time for Jimmy Collins to graduate from Commonwealth College. He had passed all of the finals and was becoming a state certified mortician. There was a big graduation party happening for him and I wanted to be there. He had sure been there for me enough times. I had a sitter for the kids that night and I brought Rhonda with me to the party. It was a nice party, plenty of drinking, dancing and lots of good food. I was never much of a dancer and so Rhonda and I just socialized and sat and watched the others dance. Jimmy had put himself through school while working full time and yet had found the time to be our body guard in his spare time. He had sure saved the day for us a few times, like back when he met Jere' under the bridge and took the kids and hid them from the F.B.I. and then again when he pulled Tim off my back when Sandy and her friends were here trying to steal them. Were it not for Jimmy, they probably would have gotten Melissa out of there that day.

By this time, Rhonda and Debbie knew who each other were because we had all lived at the same apartment complex, but they had had no reason to ever meet. Rhonda and I were sitting at a table when Jenny came up and asked me if I would please dance with Debbie. I told her that I was sorry, but no, it wouldn't be appropriate under the circumstances and I don't dance anyway. I thought that the move was a bit bold, even by Jenny's standards but I said nothing else about it.

A little while later, Rhonda excused herself and went to the ladies room. It wasn't long before a yelling match ensued from within the restroom. As all heads turned to see what was happening, Debbie came running out of the restroom with Rhonda steaming right behind her. Rhonda had seen and had evidently heard Jenny try her best to get me to dance with Debbie and she took offense to it in a very big way. I did not know that she had heard Jenny at all, Jenny had been almost whispering, nor did I notice that Rhonda had followed Debbie into the restroom to give her a piece of her mind about it. But she had.

Rhonda and I got out of there immediately, avoiding an inevitable fight between the two or maybe even between the three of them, counting Jenny. I could understand Rhonda's position on the whole thing that night and yet I knew that it was not Debbie who had started things; it was her supposed friend. I told Rhonda that I was proud of her and I told myself that I had a great big problem. A woman fighting over me scared the shit out of me and made me take a good look at what I was doing.

I began to cool things down with Rhonda in the weeks to follow. It simply came down to Rhonda caring enough about me to want to fight for me and me realizing that she wanted and deserved more than I was willing to give. She was ready to marry and settle down again and I was years into my independence with no one to answer to and no one to tell me what to do or when to do it. She deserved more from me. She deserved better than me. I knew that she would make some lucky man a terrific wife, and I knew that it wouldn't be me.

I turned it down gradually to the point where she knew that something was wrong or something had happened. One day I told her that I wanted to be alone again. I told her that I loved her and I meant it, I did love her. I loved her for all of the things she had done for us. I loved her for how she loved my children, how she gave them what they needed from a mother's side, how she showed so much patience and understanding with the three of us. I loved her for all of the wrong reasons. I couldn't continue a relationship with such a wonderful girl and cheat her out of being loved for the right reasons. I was not ready to give up my freedom and I didn't know if I ever would be ready and she deserved someone who would. She deserved someone who could love her just for her, not for how she treated his kids or how she made things convenient for him. Rhonda was very close to my kids and very close to my family, especially my sister and my parents. Linda and Rhonda wrote to each other a lot, keeping in contact long after I ended the relationship. It was a difficult time for all of us, the kids asking if Rhonda and the boys were coming over, Missy relentlessly asking if she could call Rhonda. Hell, I was missing her and her boys too. But I stuck to it, dragging her along would be unfair to her and holding on would have been for my benefit only, and it would have stopped her from finding someone better. I closed the door for good and it hurt all of us.

About six weeks later there was a knock at the door late one night, it must have been about 10 p.m. because the kids were asleep upstairs. Rhonda was at the door, dressed finer than I had ever seen her, a new red dress, hair done and all made up. She had a bottle of wine with her. She said that if it was over, she wanted one more night, a night that we would both remember.

We sat and talked, drank some wine and went through the good and bad of it all. We reminisced about how we had met and all that we had been through together. We talked about how much we both meant to each other and to each other's children. We went over the custody fight and court battles and how lucky we had been. She was such a good person that I almost agreed to pick up where we left off. But I held my own that night out of respect for her; I just couldn't lead her on any longer. I told her that it was over for good, and for her sake. I told her that I would never marry again and that she needed to find someone that would marry her and love her just for being her. I have never seen her since that night, but I have always wondered if she wound up happy. I hope so; she was one of the nicest, kindest and most considerate people that ever touched our lives and she deserved to be happy.

A couple of months later, my old friends Jenny and Harry invited me over to their house for about the hundredth time for a wine and cheese get-together one evening and this time they refused take no for an answer. I told them that I had no sitter and couldn't make it. Later that evening they called and browbeat me into going and bringing the kids with me and I said that I would, but just for a few minutes. There weren't many people there that we knew, but Debbie and her daughter Heather were there. It turned out that they had moved in with Jenny and Harry some time ago for financial reasons. I found out that Debbie and Heather were miserable there and desperately needed some help, so I asked them to come over to our house for a little while. We said our goodbyes and left and had Debbie and Heather follow a few minutes later.

We made popcorn and watched a movie together that evening and I think it got the two girls' minds away from their problems for a while. We all had a good time and I think that Debbie and Heather went home feeling a little better.

As fate would have it, I took the kids to Burger King one day a week or two later, and who should pull in just as we were getting out of our car but Debbie and Heather. It was an omen, I guess. We all sat together. And I have no earthly idea why, but it felt right.

Debbie and I slowly began to see each other after that

encounter, brief meetings at first and then to having them over to watch movies with us on weekends. It progressed into having Heather watch the kids on occasion so that Debbie and I could go out. We weren't drinkers, so going out meant going to a movie or an obligatory office function for her. Debbie and Heather had moved in with Jenny and Harry due to money problems and she was embarrassed about it. Anytime we could get the two of them over to our house, it got them out of Jenny's house. Debbie worked for Jenny and Jenny not only determined Debbie's pay, she also dictated what Debbie was to do and when she was to do it.

Debbie and I got along fine, as did the kids. Melissa was thrilled to have Heather around, sort of a big sister thing. We also learned that we had quite a bit in common, we had both been through an ugly divorce and neither of us was willing to go through it again.

On Thanksgiving Day of 1986, Debbie and Heather moved in with us. Debbie was almost broke, she was working two jobs and they were miserable living with Jenny and Harry. We, on the other hand, had a two-story house with lots of room and I was making a pretty good living. I thought what the heck, we can try this until we know whether it could work or not. We soon found out that it wouldn't be easy. Heather was 14, Brian 13 and Missy 11. The only one of the children that was happy about the whole thing was Missy, she had never had a big sister before and now she did, complete with all kinds of cool clothes that she could borrow. Heather was like Madonna to Missy, an idol. Brian was not happy about it but he put up no big fight and Heather appeared to be against it too, but willing to put forth an effort to make it work. I think that she figured it couldn't be any worse than what they had.

Things were anything but ideal in the home though. I wasn't in the habit of answering to anyone, nor were the kids used to being told what to do by someone that wasn't even family. And I had my own unrealistic expectations, like all three kids having all the chores done by the time Debbie and I got home. And Debbie wasn't exactly used to coming home from work and cooking either, and Heather was spoiled rotten, getting pretty much anything that she wanted whenever she wanted it, as long as it shut her up and kept her happy.

Debbie had married young, just as I did, at 18 years old. Pregnant at the wedding, she realized quickly that this marriage was not meant to be. It lasted less than a year and then Debbie and Heather were on their own. They had moved to Texas years ago to make a better life for themselves and Debbie was working two jobs trying to make it happen. She had become as used to being independent as I had and getting her to trust me and share her problems with me was a tough sell. And I was still the "I can do it all guy," a single parent now for over five years and not really needing anyone's help. I was blessed with the ability to make a good living and thankfully, at least in my case, being a mom and a dad to two kids was not as hard as people seemed to think it was.

We had a great Christmas that year. Having been together only four or five weeks, we hadn't had time to develop interpersonal likes and dislikes yet. But things began to get a little rougher for us after the first of the year of 1987. It turned out that things the kids and I liked to do, Debbie and Heather didn't and vice versa. It was goodbye to the Tuesday night pizza get-togethers with Jeb and Grace, Joe and Pety and their families. We needed to adjust our lives and our money and compensate accordingly. All of us expected things at first that were unrealistic and we went through a period of adjustment for the first four months of that year.

I had this stupid expectation that I would come home from work and find supper ready and a loving family there, all happily waiting to see me. Why not? It had been forever since I had been able to enjoy things like that and besides, I wanted it. Debbie, on the other hand didn't get home any sooner than I did and had no time to give me those things, let alone the fact that she didn't have any idea what I was expecting, anyway.. And that wasn't her fault; she had been single longer than I had. The kids, well, let's just say that they didn't want to share rooms and they certainly did not want to share chores. Brian had to move out of the biggest bedroom upstairs and go to the smaller one so that the two girls could share the bigger room. That didn't make him too happy at all. They were beginning to get on each other's nerves more and more each day. Heather seemed to have so much going on all the time that she just didn't have time for chores and sitting at the dining room table with my kids doing homework was not something she cared to do, something else that I expected. Trying to get the three of them all on an even level was tough enough, but trying to get Heather to realize that she was no longer an only child, that she now had a brother and little sister, was rough. Missy was tall for her age, as tall as Heather, so Missy could wear quite a few of Heather's things. The only problem was that Heather wouldn't let her, so she would do it without asking. Heather would look for something and find out that Missy had it, yell at her mother, who would in turn rag on me about the whole mess. "Your daughter is out of control," she would say to me. "What the hell are you talking about?" I would answer. "Little sisters do that kind of thing all the time, it's no big deal."

And then there were the times when Debbie would call me at work to tell me that we were going out that night with Jenny and Harry and I would take offense to someone planning my time for me. I can plan my own time, thank you and I can also pick who I want to socialize with. Debbie worked for Jenny and what Jenny wanted from her employees and friends, Jenny got. I, on the other hand, didn't work for her and she was not, nor ever had been, one of my favorite friends. I was less than happy with her for starting that damn fiasco at Jimmy's graduation party and for the way she would keep Debbie smashed under her thumb. So when Debbie would call me in a panic about how Jenny wanted this, or Jenny wanted that, I would pretty much say I don't give a damn. Let's say that I was less than understanding about a lot of things. I wasn't used to giving in and I wasn't used to sharing, just like the kids. Debbie would beg me to go here with them, or do this or that with them, but I read Jenny right the first time I ever saw her, a bossy woman who demanded her way from everyone. She wasn't on my list of favorite people. And each time I said no, Debbie feared the repercussions and she would be stuck between the man she lived with and the wrath of the woman that she worked for. I understand her dilemma now, although back then I didn't and I didn't give a damn, either.

By the summer of the year we were fighting like cats and dogs. Debbie would come home and do the things you need to do after a long hard day at work and I would grab my kids and head out the door to go get something to eat. No one was making any attempt to make a meal, including myself, so we'd just go get one somewhere. Debbie would get furious with my expecting her to come home from work and make supper for us and my getting pissed when she didn't. To really make a point one time, I just grabbed my kids and left, letting her figure the rest out. I was a perfect asshole. One day she threw a box of frozen broccoli at me as I was going out the door, hitting me right in the head. Things were just plain shitty and I wasn't going to let us live this way after everything we had been through and this was not what we had fought for. I decided that I would just go buy a house and leave Debbie and Heather at the rent house and I would pay a few months rent ahead for them. I was tired of the whining between the kids, the "he won't do his chores," "she's wearing my sweater again," or the "how come she doesn't have to do anything?" stuff, all that crap. And I was tired of the fighting, tired of sleeping in the same bed with someone and yet not speaking to each other. It's hard to fall asleep with your chest pounding in frustration and God forbid that you accidentally touch the other one; it would be misconstrued as a sign of weakness or of giving in to the other.

Over a period of a few weeks I went out and looked at about 40 HUD homes and found one that I thought would be great for us. I put in a bid on it and after a few attempts, I got it. After I had signed the papers and really owned the house, I told Debbie about it. I told her that the kids and I were moving, Heather and she were not. I would pay the rent ahead three months and we would be moving out. The fighting would be over, the battle lost by both sides. But we put forth a good effort and gave it our best shot. It was just not meant to be.

Well, the shit hit the fan and we had it out that night, all night. It was ugly! Her view of the situation differed greatly from my view. Debbie got so upset about it that she went out onto the back patio and stayed out there on a chaise lounge for almost three days, coming in only to use the bathroom or to get something to eat or drink. And then she finally came in and told me that she realized that she wanted to be with me and "if that meant doing things your way, then that's what it meant." She said that she was willing to do whatever I wanted, however I wanted, just to stay with me. That really made me think about what it was that I really wanted. It's funny; I realized that all I really wanted from her was an even playing field for the kids, all three of them all treated the same and loved the same by both of us.

In August of 1987 we moved into our new home together, the five of us. It wasn't a big house, but it had a swimming pool in the back and that's what all three kids liked the most. We made the front formal room into a bedroom and each kid now had their own room. Things began to get better immediately. I know it sounds like I broke Debbie's spirit and things were getting better because I was getting my way, but that's not the truth. I did not ask Debbie to change, nor did I try to break her spirit, I wanted us to be a family, not two families living under one roof like it had been. I began to change the way I thought about things, too. I loved her, but I had not been considerate of her until now.

For Christmas of 1987, we made plans for all of us to go to Pennsylvania; it would be our first trip home since we left six years ago and the family could meet Debbie and Heather. We were going to drive up because flying five of us round-trip was more than we could afford. Driving would be all right I thought, as long as we didn't get pulled over anywhere while I was driving and as long as we avoided Ohio altogether. I was still wanted, the warrant old now but still valid. If stopped anywhere else I figured that I could show them my court papers and not be bothered. I wanted my parents to meet Debbie and Heather as soon as possible. I wanted the girls to see where we came from, to play in the snow and enjoy the fun and meet my family and I really wanted to go home. And besides, nothing had happened relating to Sandy in more than a year, so I figured that no one cared anymore. As it got closer to Christmas, Debbie told me that she couldn't get the time off from work. Jenny was making things difficult for her, probably because I had squeezed her out of our lives. I was upset about it and told Debbie to come along anyway and to quit her lousy job when we got back, but she wouldn't. She wasn't ready to do battle with Jenny, nor was she willing to surrender her independence and allow me to be the sole breadwinner, the supreme leader of the family. She wasn't going and that was that. Now we were going without her and to make it worse, we weren't even speaking again. Just before we were about to pull out, Debbie got in her car and left, nothing spoken, she just left. The rest of us, Heather included, finished packing up and we drove off leaving Debbie alone for Christmas. As the kids and I drove towards the freeway, we saw Debbie parked at a nearby gas station waiting for us to pass by because she couldn't bear to be at home when we left. It was really sad leaving without her, but as time went on the kids and I learned to make the most of it. We had roughly 1,500 miles or so to drive and I was the only driver, none of the kids were old enough to drive yet. The weather was horrible for almost the entire trip. We had to stop in Memphis the first night. After being run off the highway by an 18-wheeler that slid in the snow, I had to ditch into the center median to avoid him and it scared us to death. I was already tired and I figured that 600 miles that day was good enough. It didn't help that the check engine light had come on in the car and the defroster had stopped working, the windshield becoming almost impossible to see through because it was so cold out. All we did was shower, eat and sleep and we were gone early the next morning.

The next day, we drove the rest of the way, stopping only for restroom breaks, gas, food and coffee. I was getting very tired and the three kids decided that the best way to keep me from falling asleep was to sing Christmas carols together. It was wonderful; we must have driven the last 300 miles just singing songs. It was snowing like crazy as we drove north on I- 79 towards Erie, Pennsylvania and Heather had never seen so much snow before, making it was a real experience for her. We managed to do over 900 miles that day and make it home.

Being at Mom and Dad's house again was surreal for us. We hadn't been home at all since the night that I carried the kids out the door and drove away in 1981. I thought of all the experiences we had lived through since then and all of the good times we had shared. I thought of how much we would have missed and how many friends we would never have met if we had never left at all. And then I thought about all of the things that we had missed up there while we were gone.

All of the family gathered together, everyone wanting to hear all of our stories and to get to know Heather and reconnect with Brian and Missy again. It was a good time, but still, we were sad inside about leaving Debbie alone for Christmas and sad that she was not with us to share the experience. It was snowing like crazy and playing in it was a lot of fun, the kids were making snow angels and all of us were having snowball fights. We went over to my brother Alan's house and we were making popcorn balls and we were all just staying warm by the fire and enjoying the family. We were keeping our presence a secret for the most part, knowing that there was a chance that I could be arrested and the kids taken if the wrong people found out that we were there. Alan lived only about three miles from the Ohio state line. Sometime that evening, my father took a phone call at Alan's house and said that he had to go and that he would be back as soon as he could. I had no idea what he needed to do that couldn't wait until after the snow let up, but it was none of my business and so I said nothing other than to tell him to be careful. He reminded me that they live there and deal with the weather every day.

Hours later we were all looking at family pictures when we heard my father come in, the excitement in his voice betraying him right away. He had Debbie with him. The phone call he took was from Debbie, she was calling from the bus station in Erie, a good 30 miles away. She had been standing at the bus stop for hours, she said, trying to find a way to reach my father at home, but we were all at Alan's house. Debbie had felt so bad about staying behind that she had hopped a bus in Houston and had traveled for 44 hours to get there and surprise us. And she did this while having the flu. I have had many surprises in my life, but her coming up on a bus alone and sick was one of the best surprises ever; it showed a commitment to me and even more importantly, to us as a family. We had the absolute best time of our lives together, playing in the snow, chatting with family and thanking them all for the parts that they had played in making our lives what they were. The trip was the best time we had ever had as a complete family and having Debbie with us on the way back was icing on the cake. We had no trouble at all up there as far as the law went; no one knew we had been there until after we were gone. And the trip home was fine and it's always good to be home, no matter where you have been. We passed a hurdle together on that trip and our lives together would be better after that. I guess we finally bonded as a family.

Things didn't go that well the next time we went home though. On October 9th, 1988, my parents would be celebrating their 40th wedding anniversary and Alan and Linda were throwing a surprise party for them and we were invited. But this time Debbie and Heather could not go with us. After having such a good experience the last time we went home, we mistakenly felt that things would be all right if we went up for the big surprise party.

My aunt and uncle from England that were at Mom and Dad's when we first left in 1981 were coming over for the party and all my brothers, now scattered across the country would be there too, it was going to be a big bash. I bought round-trip tickets for the three of us and we flew into Cleveland, Ohio, and rented a car. It was about 80 miles from the airport to my parents' house just inside the Pennsylvania State line. I had reservations about going into Ohio, but it had been five years since they had looked for me last and besides, we were there last Christmas and no one seemed to care anymore.

We weren't at my parents' house two hours before I made the fateful mistake of answering the phone. I shouldn't have. I was just excited to be there. I answered by saying "Hello?" and whoever it was said "Hello", (in a very warm family type way), "who's this?" Without hesitating or giving it a thought, I said "Glen, who's this?" And they hung up. Less than four hours later the Pennsylvania State police were at the door asking my father if we were there. My father was an honest man, I know, very unusual for a car salesman, right? He was, and rather than tell them no, he asked why they were asking. The policemen told Dad that I was wanted in Ohio, and Ohio had reason to believe that I was there and had asked them for help in finding out. My younger brother, Jack, up from Florida for the occasion, intervened, not the least bit intimidated by them and unafraid to lie to them. He told them that they hadn't seen us and that they knew for a fact that we were not coming. The State Police then asked if they could come in and have a look around the house and then be on their way. Brother Jack told them that they could not; this was a family get-together for a special occasion and they were not going to ruin things. The policemen said that they could go get a search warrant and come back if they had to and Brother Jack told them that that was exactly what they would have to do if they wanted to come in. His words were more like "Fucking pigs, why don't you go fuck with some real criminals instead of trying to find out who's pissing in the snow?" The officers at the door got pretty offended and vowed to be back with a search warrant. Jack told them to do whatever they felt they needed to do, but that "*there ain't no donuts in here* so why waste your time?" You would have to know my brother Jack to understand him. He's a year younger than I and as we were growing up he showed little regard for his own safety; he was pretty much fearless and reckless. He had grown up to be six-foot-two, 270 pounds and was absolutely unafraid of anyone or anything. After a stint in the Navy, he had settled in Jacksonville, Florida, married a local girl and raised a family there. Jack is the kind that will say anything he feels like saying, anywhere, anytime. He is the kind that could walk into a strange bar and say, "who stinks, somebody in here stinks and I don't want to smell shit while I drink. So whoever it is, get your nasty ass out of here."

Don't misunderstand him, he doesn't really look for trouble, okay, at least not anymore, he just says what he thinks when he thinks it. He has a very big heart to go with his big size. He is a motor home mechanic by trade and now has his own company out in Savannah, Georgia.

When the policemen at the door left, they stationed two patrol cars out in front of my parents' house, evidently to make sure that I didn't leave if I was inside. And we were, I was hiding on the floor in my parent's bedroom and the kids had been whisked into the bedroom closet. The lights were deliberately turned off so that no one could see anything inside and the whole family was now deeply involved in the action. Even the ones from England were involved now, as if caught up in a crime novel. The police were parked outside and were now walking around the perimeter of the house, either gathering information about exit routes or else just making sure that we didn't sneak out through a window. We all knew that we had to do something before they came back and a lot of suggestions were mulled over in the darkness of that house. In that darkness you could smell both the fear and the excitement.

We agreed on a plan, actually I didn't agree on anything, the kids and I were kept out of the process, in hiding and afraid the police would hear our voices if we so much as spoke. My family came up with a plan and it was impressive; there were 16 of us in the house and four cars in the driveway. And there were two police cars out front on Route 20. At exactly the same time, all 16 of us would run out of the door and get into the four cars, four people to a car and every car would bolt out of the driveway going the three possible different directions!

It was the best that they could do; the police would show up with a search warrant almost anytime now and I would go to jail, probably for years. The kids would go to their mother, still the last place that they wanted to be, and the anniversary party would be a disaster.

We hit the door and went four to a car with only the driver showing in each car, everyone else ducked down below window level. Four cars pulled out and went three different directions, one North on Nye Road, another one West and two cars East on Route 20. The two police cars couldn't cover all four cars and not all of them were in their cars. One followed North and the other one opted to go the same direction as the two of our cars that headed east towards Erie and away from the Ohio state line. The car we were in, headed West and towards Ohio and being driven by my brother Alan, was not followed. They did follow my father's car and he proceeded to drive north towards Lake Erie. After my father had stopped along the shore of the lake, the police pulled up behind him and after thoroughly looking in his car, asked him exactly what he was doing. Father told them that the family members from England had wanted to see Lake Erie at night. Mother later told me that while speaking to the police, Dad was wearing the biggest smile that she had ever seen on his face.

We had to go where they would not think to look for us, and since my brother Alan was driving, he took us about 45 miles away to the home of his in-laws, Mr. and Mrs. Roy Ritter in Greenville, Pennsylvania. I had had the pleasure of meeting them long before and they knew me and a little bit about our situation. They kindly offered their home to us. Thanks to the Ritter family, we had a place to stay while we decided how to get home.

The evening after our escape was the party for my parents. The kids and I stayed in Greenville while the rest of them went to the party that evening. Of course the police showed up at the party looking for me and it really put a damper on the night, although the family tried their best to make the most of it. One of my biggest disappointments is how I ruined that week and that special night for my folks. My father would pass away before their 50th anniversary, so knowing that I lessened the pleasure of their 40th is something that will always bother me.

We knew that we could not go back to Cleveland and use our round-trip tickets; by now they surely knew that we were there and how we got there, so they would probably be watching for us at the airport. We had to figure out another way to get home to Houston. And the longer we took, the more time they had to cover all of the bases and find us.

What I decided to do was use phony names and buy one-way tickets to Houston and fly out of Pittsburgh. Alan and Jeanne checked on flights out of Pittsburgh while the rest of us, Linda and Mike, my brothers and the three of us all waited at a nearby restaurant. Alan and Jeanne came back saying that there was a flight to Houston leaving in two hours and it was not booked full. Together, we agreed that it was the best way out and before the kids and I went into the airport, my brothers all went in looking for any signs that law enforcement was there looking for us. With a green light from the family, we all went in together and approached the ticket counter. I told them that we had an emergency on our hands and that we had to fly to Houston, one-way, as soon as possible. I told them that my name was David Adams, my son's name was Thomas and my daughter's name was Kathy. In truth, back in Houston I worked with a friend named Dave Adams and he had two children. To this day we still work together. We did not have to show any identification back then to buy a ticket, so I paid for them in cash. It was then that they asked me if we were checking any bags and I said yes. That's when they asked for identification, if you were checking bags you had to show them your identification. The whole group of us looked at each other and for a second, we thought for sure that we were screwed. My brothers quickly said that they would send our baggage to us by other means. Brother Gary just looked at the girl and said, "They won't have time when they land to bother with luggage, so no, they won't be checking any bags." We left the ticket counter wondering if we had aroused the curiosity of the airline employee, but then we figured that they had probably seen everything before.

The family walked down to the gate first, making sure all was safe. They were thorough in their search, looking for any sign of law enforcement, but came back and gave the okay, so we said our goodbyes and gave thanks and after waiting until the last minute, we boarded. We were all scared shitless, every one of us, and getting on that plane was one of the hardest things I have ever done. I was convinced that we would be caught. I could see Sandy in the back of my mind, standing in the airport giving me the finger again and I could visualize the kids crying as they were being dragged, not wanting to go with her. My family should receive an award of merit for the way that they scoured that airport inside and out before waving us in and onto the plane. Goodbyes were quick and driven by panic and fear. Linda was bawling.

We were the last ones to board the plane and with no bags we were in seats quickly, even though someone else was in one of our seats. No time to argue or bring ourselves any unwanted attention, I thought. We had waited until last because I wanted to see if there was any kind of activity going on that looked unusual to me. If anything looked strange at all, we would just walk away. We'd find another way home, train maybe. So we waited and boarded last. And because someone was in one of our seats, I sat in an empty seat directly in front of Brian and Melissa, I mean Thomas and Kathy. I was looking at my watch, counting the few seconds until our scheduled departure time, wondering if the kids could remember their aliases if asked their names. The departure time came and went. And we waited, and we waited. Oh God, they know we're here. We've been caught, I thought. The authorities are at the gate and in a minute we will be arrested and taken off the plane, all three of us in hand-cuffs this time. To make it this long and then get caught because of my stupidity was a horrible thing, I thought.

"Attention passengers," the intercom said, "we have a short delay, we apologize for any inconvenience and we will be on our way momentarily."

I couldn't even sit still; my breathing was in gasps now, my whole body shaking. The lady next to me, an older woman, asked me if it was my first time flying and without hesitating I told her that it was. She put her hand on top of mine on the armrest and assured me that I would be fine. "Relax and take deep breaths," she said, trying to comfort me. Thanks lady, I thought to myself, you have no idea how much that means to me right now.

The kids were afraid too. My panic was obvious and my daughter started crying. I could do little to help as I was virtu-ally frozen with fear, my eyes riveted on the entrance to the plane. The stillness and the silence were suffocating me. I needed air, I needed an escape hatch. Time was standing still and my heart was slamming against my ribcage. "Please Lord," I said to myself, "I will pay you back forever if you help us right now."

And then there was some commotion in the front of the plane. "Ladies and gentlemen," the intercom spewed, "we are cleared for takeoff," and right then the plane started moving. I knew that if we got off the ground we would most likely be safe. The odds of them turning around for a kidnapper were what? 50-50?

The plane soared down the runway and when I realized that we were airborne, I began to cry. The nice lady next to me put her hand on mine again and said, "I told you that it would be fine and see, it is." I looked behind me and both children were grinning from ear to ear, my daughter saying "Daddy, its okay now, please don't cry." The lady next to me was right, it would be fine, but if she only knew. I thanked her for her support in my time of need, it was very comforting. And then I thanked God, again and again and again. I still do.

CHAPTER FOURTEEN:
IN RETROSPECT

In 1990, my Uncle Richard passed away back home and I couldn't go. I wasn't going to put my children or my family through that again. I vowed to do something legally so that we could go back home and not have to worry. Since I couldn't go home for the funeral, I wrote a poem about my Uncle Dick, my father's youngest brother, and I sent it up there. I didn't expect them to read it at the services, but they did, and finding that out made me feel like I had been there. I guess I was, at least in spirit.

That same year, Brian left and went up to spend most of the year living with his mother. He wanted to get away from what he felt were overly strict rules in our home, but I think that deep down he just wanted to get to know his mother and see what life was like with her. He found out after a while that there are reasons for rules. Parents don't just come up with rules to make children miserable; they do it to make children into better people. Discipline is not a form of punishment; it is a form of love. Tough love sometimes, but love.

After Brian came back in 1991, he got into trouble when he started running with a bad crowd and he quit school. After pleading with him to straighten out and stay in school, he quit anyway, and when he did I threw him out of my house. And when he wound up needing a lawyer after getting in trouble with that bad crowd, I was so mad at him that I refused to get one for him, although I wish now that I had. Anyway, he paid his dues and never once blamed anyone but himself. He received his G.E.D. years ago and is now attending a Community College and only a few credits shy of his degree.

In July of 1992, with the help of attorney William Bobulsky, a motion to dismiss was filed in Ashtabula, Ohio. There was no response from my ex-wife, her attorney or the state, and all charges against me were dismissed for want of prosecution. For the first time in 11 years, I could go home and not worry about being arrested.

That same summer my daughter ran away from home. It was a terrible time for us. I was posting her picture on convenience store doors and driving around every evening trying to find her. I knew from outside sources that she was all right; she was staying with different friends and moving around just out of my reach. I would meet friends of ours over on Westheimer, the main street that crosses the city and the place where everything you wanted to find could be found. We would split up every evening and search. Search every club, cool hangout, restaurant, and movie theater that we could find. Friends like Jerry Brown (known as the governor to us), Todd Keel, Joe Serrano, Dennis Kitelinger, Donny Hagle and Dave Adams, people who cared about us and took the time to help me search for her. Now would be a good time to thank all of our friends who, not for the first time, put my family first and helped us when we needed help.

When I did finally get word where she was staying, I sat outside of the apartment until I saw her go in; it was a heart-wrenching experience. As soon as I saw her I called the local police and had them meet me there and they went in and extracted her and we brought her home against her will. But it didn't last and soon after, she ran away again and this time I got a call from her mother saying that she was with her in Ohio. Melissa said that we were being too tough with her, too restrictive and so she decided to see how living with her mother would be. I was absolutely, thoroughly disheartened by the problems with both of the kids. After all that we had been through, after we bought her the car that she left in, for her to want to run away broke my heart. But it didn't take long before Melissa called me and said that she had made a big mistake and wanted to come home, just like her brother. Since I am the asshole that I am, I told her that it would do her some good to stay there for her senior year and get to know her mother. She told me that she knew enough already and begged me to let her come home, but I was pissed and even though it was hard, I told her no.

That Christmas Debbie and I drove home and my daughter came to my parents' house to see us. It was an ugly situation. I didn't know how to act. I was bitter about her running away from me and she was bitter because I wouldn't let her come home. My children had been my entire life and any price I had paid to be with them was well worth it, but to have her treat me like that really tore me up inside. As hard as it was, we left her there and the following spring she graduated from Ashtabula High School. We drove up for it; I had gotten over being mad at her and was feeling a huge void in my life. I knew that graduating was a big moment in her life and I wanted to surprise her by being there. And it was good to be able to go back and forth now. Just to stand in my parents' house, the home I had grown up in, without the fear of being arrested, was worth the price I paid to get the charges dismissed. We drove back to Houston with Melissa with us. Her graduation gift from me was my saying that I was sorry and that I loved her, missed her and wanted her to come back home. That made us all happy.

On Fathers' day of 1997 I was opening a Fathers' Day card from my daughter when my brother Alan called. "Happy Father's day," I told him. "Thanks," he said, "but you need to come home right away." "Right away meaning now?" I asked. "Now," he said, "Dad is in bad shape and they don't expect him to make it, his heart is giving out fast."

I had Debbie and Melissa call airlines as I packed a bag and we left for the airport as soon as I had showered. I flew into Cleveland and rented a car to get to the hospital in Conneaut, a 75-mile drive that took me less than an hour. It was the same hospital that I had been police escorted to 22 years earlier for the birth of my daughter.

I did get to see my father for a while before he passed away, most of us did make it home in time. He would drift in and out of consciousness and one particular time he looked up at all of us as we stood there surrounding his bed and he asked us how long he had. Linda said, "Not long dad." "So," he said "I guess it's time to say *goodbye* then." And for the first time in our lives we heard him say the word *goodbye* to each of us, one by one, calling us by name and shaking our hand. This time it would not be the "*see you later*," or the "*so long for now*," the words that we were so accustomed to hearing from him. And then he fell asleep and shortly after, peacefully passed away. The man who had made me what I am, the man who had a heart as big as Texas and had passed it on to his children, was gone. I watched him take his last breath and while kissing him on his forehead, I promised him and the Lord both that I would carry on his generosity and kindness and help as many people as I could, just like him.

The next evening as I was sitting on Mom and Dad's front porch, the words to a poem began to take shape in my head and by the next evening I had it down and ready to read at his funeral; I called it...

"Safe Passage"
Although it is always sought it just cannot be bought,
this ticket was earned by your choices each day.
If you have one you're greeted, no passport is needed,

the angels will show you the way.
Safe passage is granted to only a few
and the Heavens will open to a spectacular view.
I know God gave safe passage to Dad,
there is no need to be sad;
His path lit by the light of the stars.
He is in heaven today, where he's having his way
and no doubt, he is still selling cars.

Copyright © 1997.

One day in March of 1999 Debbie asked me to stop at a motorcycle dealership that we were passing. As we walked through the showroom, she asked me which one I would want if I was going to buy one. I pointed at a black Valkyrie with windshield and saddlebags and said that it would be the perfect bike for us when we're ready to get one. She walked straight over to a salesman, pointed to the bike and said, "We'll take that one," and two hours later I drove it home. She said that I had waited long enough and that she wanted me to have it and that was that. Eighteen years after I lost everything that I had, it had now all been replaced.

My son met the love of his life, Mynda Pridgen, and they were married in July of 1999 in Humble, Texas. My mother was healthy enough to be able to come down for the wedding. While she was here, I had the opportunity to show her the internet for the first time in her life and she was absolutely thrilled. I showed her a live camera shot of Weymouth beach in England, the town where she lived during World War II and the place where she had met my father. Two of her sisters still live there today. I also managed to pull up pictures of Jersey, in the Channel Islands, her birthplace. Mom was beside herself after getting to see so much of her past.

Sandy and Ralph were also here for the big event. Sandy, Brian and Melissa all came by my office one day to pick me up for lunch while she was here. It was quite strange to have all four of us together in one car for the first time in over 18 years. As we were driving to the restaurant my son let out a resounding laugh and said he had been waiting all his life to say, "Mom, Dad, are we there yet?" It really broke the ice and melted away the years and the bitterness and we all laughed.

We had a good meal that day and as we were walking back to the car, Sandy gingerly put her hand on my arm and asked me why I did it, why I took the kids so long ago. I told her that I did what I felt was best for them under the circumstances at the time and I told her to take a good look at our children and tell me that I had made a mistake or that I had done a poor job of raising them. "Tell me that you could have done better," I said. "Look at what they went through as they tried to get to know you." She said absolutely nothing, and I opened the door for her.

At the wedding Sandy and I had to walk down the aisle together arm in arm. It was a very strange thing. As I walked down the aisle with her I thought about how in love we were all those years ago when we eloped. She let out a laugh and said that it felt like the wedding that we never had. It was a wonderful wedding, most of the family came down and everything went very well. By the time that Sandy left, there were no longer any ill feelings between us. We had found common ground and the peace that comes with it and we had two children that we were both extremely proud of.

On December 29th of that same year, my daughter called me at work and said that her mother was sick and that she wished she could get up to see her, but it was too expensive to fly on short notice and she couldn't afford to take the time off anyhow. I offered to pay for her ticket and she decided that she and Brian would wait to hear if Sandy got any better or not before they made any decisions. The next morning Melissa called me again, this time with news that her mother was no better and that they needed to go. I told her that I hoped to hear good news from them soon and to keep me posted. Tickets were purchased and the kids packed and left for the airport to catch the flight. I checked on them from time to time by way of cell phones and their flight wound up delayed due to bad weather in Cleveland. About two hours went by and then I got a call at my office from up north with the news that Sandy had passed away. They wanted me to decide whether to tell the kids or not before they left. Judging by the amount of time that the kids had been waiting at the airport here in Houston and the possibility that someone else might call them and tell them, I felt it best to drive the 50 miles to the airport and tell them myself.

As I walked toward the terminal I could see the three of them standing outside of the entrance so that my daughter could smoke. When I got about 100 yards from them they recognized me and it took just a split second for them to realize that there was only one reason why I would be there. They started saying no before I could get to them and when I did, I pulled them together in a big bear hug and told them that their mother had passed. I had to; allowing them to think all the way up there that their mother would be glad to see them was, in my opinion, the wrong way to do it. We stood there crying together, all of us in one big hug, until the reality of it had set in and they began to settle down. Shortly after, they boarded the plane and left. Watching them walk through the gate that day was horrible. I was their daddy and there was no way for me to take away their pain.

Sandy died of the flu; it had brought about pneumonia and death at the age of 49. It was just a day before the big Y2K thing. It must have been a very sad flight home for them. I stood there until the plane was out of my sight. After that I called up north and told them that the kids had been told and that no one up there would have to be the bearer of the news. I also told the kids that I would fly up for the funeral if they thought it proper or if they thought they needed me in any way, but they felt that it would not be appropriate and I had to agree. It was a good thing Brian married when he did, we learned that anything can happen in a span of six months.

On December 22nd, 2001 I got the call that my mother was in bad shape. She had been in the hospital for about a week with all of the signs of end stage heart failure. We knew that she was going downhill, but we didn't expect what was about to happen. I had taken Christmas week off for vacation and had my tickets in hand to fly up there on Christmas Eve. But the call came to come home now, so once again Debbie and my daughter made flight arrangements while I packed and as soon as I was ready, they took me to the airport and dropped me off. It was the very same airport that I had flown out of when my father died and the very airport where I had told the kids about their mother. I hate that airport now; for me it reeks with death. I can't walk into it for any reason without thinking about all of them.

I was waiting at the gate to board the plane when my cell phone rang. I didn't want to answer it, but I knew that I had to. It was my brother-in-law, Michael, and as he told me that my mother had just passed away, I felt this overwhelming sadness, this feeling of complete helplessness that I had never felt before. Standing in line to board, I started shaking as if I was in zero degree weather. When the reality of it all hit me and the crying began, the people around me started staring at me and then the airline employees came. I guess that they thought that I was on drugs or having some sort of a medical emergency because they walked me out of the line and started asking me all kinds of questions. I told them why I was upset and with their condolences and the normal, "If there is anything we can do, please let us know," they left me alone. It was a solemn flight home. The airline employees kept watch over me and kept me in coffee as I sat quietly and motionless, pondering the fact that I did not get to say goodbye to the best mother that ever lived and realizing that I was now officially an orphan. It brought me back to the poem that I had written for my mother some 20 years earlier and how much she had loved it.

The day before Mother's Day of 1980, I sat and wrote a poem for her and when finished, I rewrote it into a Mother's Day card and gave it to her. Upon reading it, she cried and said that it was the nicest thing ever given to her. I called it....

"A Mother's Day Gift"
I could have purchased something nice to give to you this day,
Flowers, books and other things; they all have words to say.
But if a picture's worth a thousand words, why do I feel the need
To tell you again I love you and I'm so proud to be your seed?
Your loving and caring and doing without as I grew through the years,
Will never be forgotten Mom, in fact, it brings me tears.
My heart is full of room for Dad and my family and friends all share,
But no one else will <u>ever</u> touch the space for you in there.

Copyright © 1980.

Mother loved that poem so much that several years later I had it engraved onto a plaque for her. I gave it to her one Christmas and she placed it on her dining room wall where it remained until her death, at which time I removed it and read

it at her funeral services. I then placed it next to her in her casket where it will be with her forever. I guarantee you that she
is proudly showing it to others in heaven today.

On February 1, 2005, Phillip Crosby passed away at his
home in Rosenberg. It was an honor for me to speak at his services and tell everyone the story of how he opened the door to
our new lives so many years ago. Yes, had this man not hired me
I would have found a job somewhere else, but our lives might
have gone in a completely different direction. We might have
wound up in another city with completely different friends and
maybe we would not have gotten the help and support needed
to keep us together. Who knows?

CHAPTER FIFTEEN:
NO REGRETS

It is now Christmas of the year 2004. Debbie and I (and our eight cats) just spent Christmas day with Brian, his wife Mynda, my grandchildren—three-year-old Emma and her four-week-old little brother Mason, Melissa, her boyfriend, Tony, and his son, Anthony. Debbie's daughter, Heather, is married and the mother of three children of her own, Payton, Nealey and Lauren, with Lauren having the dubious distinction of having been born on the very day that we buried my mother. As one precious life was ending, another was just beginning. Heather is a registered nurse in Mississippi and they couldn't be here for Christmas this year.

I must thank Debbie, who has now spent 18 years putting up with me and all that I carry with me. At this time in my life, I can honestly say that it doesn't get any better than this.

It turned out well. I am so proud of my two children that if I died today, I would feel that I accomplished what God had set out for me. Although they went through some difficult times, I could not have asked for more from them. I have two real heroes in my life, one being my father, who set such an example by his humanity and generosity that I will spend all of my life trying just to come close, and the other being my son, who shows me on a regular basis what being a good father really is. And all these years I thought that I was a pretty good father. I don't even come close to him.

I have to close by saying that what I did was wrong. I don't encourage anyone else to ever do it. This story should never have happened. But then again, I shudder to think about how our lives would be if it had never happened. I am so close to my children that I feel sorry for all parents that do not have the ties that we have. All of the things that happened in this story are true and because we could share the hard times, the good times and the help and friendship of all of the people that we encountered, we would not have it any other way. We wouldn't change a thing. I just wish I could have kept the kids eight and six years old forever. The three of us have no regrets.

As I finish this book I gaze out through a window of my now paid for home and I see my car and motorcycle, also paid for. I can remember when we first came to Houston. I can remember when we had nowhere to live and everything that we owned could fit in the backseat of a car. I think of a time when I couldn't afford to buy a cup of coffee. I think about how blessed I am at this very moment and even so, with everything I have now, even with having achieved every dream I ever had thanks to the grace of God, I wish I could trade today and go back in time to when we left. I wish we could do it all over again. I loved it that much.

May God bless you as much as he has blessed me.

Glen C. Schulz. Copyright © 2004.

Epilogue:
by Melissa

My name is Melissa, I am Glen's daughter and I have to say that there has never been a day in my whole life when I regretted what my father has done. If anything, I wish I could be eight years old again, living in a one-bedroom apartment with the two most important people in my world, my brother and my daddy. I did eventually forge a relationship with my mother; I got to know her for eight years before her untimely death. In the end there were no harsh words spoken, just a family that had finally come full circle.

Daddy, you have always been, and will always be, such an amazing man to me. You are the light in my life and you'll never know how much I love you!! I am so proud of you for everything that you have accomplished.